THE CRAWL SPACE

Don't cut the pipes

by

Sharolyn Sidebottom

TATE PUBLISHING, LLC

Published in the United States of America
By TATE PUBLISHING, LLC
All rights reserved.
Do not duplicate without permission.

All Scripture references are Amplified Version, unless otherwise indicated.

Book Design by TATE PUBLISHING, LLC.

Printed in the United States of America by
TATE PUBLISHING, LLC
127 East Trade Center Terrace
Mustang, OK 73064
(888) 361-9473

Publisher's Cataloging in Publication

Sidebottom, Sharolyn

The Crawl Space/Sharolyn Sidebottom

Originally published in Mustang,OK:TATE PUBLISHING:2004

1. Christianity 2. Family 3. Self-Help

ISBN 0-9753933-3-2 $15.95

Copyright 2004

First Printing: May 2004

Table of Contents

Prologue 5

Introduction 7

Chapter 1   Help Me! I'm Stuck In The Crawl Space 11

Chapter 2   Seasons Change In The Crawl Space 17

Chapter 3   Discovering Integrity In The Crawl Space 25

Chapter 4   Corroded Or Corrupted In The Crawl Space 41

Chapter 5   Do We Avoid Or Endure The Crawl Space? 51

Chapter 6   Becoming The Vision In The Crawl Space 57

Chapter 7   The Crawl Space Proves What We Are Made Of ... 65

Chapter 8   Surrender In The Crawl Space 75

Chapter 9   The Crawl Space Is Boot Camp 81

Chapter 10   Gideon's Crawl Space 87

Chapter 11   Joseph's Crawl Space 97

Chapter 12   Women Are Emerging From The Crawl Space 105

Chapter 13   Worship In The Crawl Space 113

Chapter 14   Seek Ye First The Kingdom Of God
             In The Crawl Space 123

Chapter 15   And Seek His Righteousness In The Crawl Space . 129

Chapter 16   Becoming An Instrument In The Crawl Space 139

Chapter 17   Measuring Up In The Crawl Space 151

Appendix   Romans Road To Righteousness 159

Prologue

In the following scripture written by James, an apostle of the Lord Jesus Christ, we find keys to becoming spiritually mature, perfectly and fully developed lacking nothing. In the pages of this book we will be exploring the purpose of trials—events of life that are hard to deal with and hard to bear—in the hope of establishing a paradigm that will enable the body of Christ to be patient under trial, standing upright under temptation, and growing in steadfast patient endurance. It is not what happens to us but what happens in us as we stand the test of time to be approved and receive the victor's crown of life. So let's read James again for the first time as he begins with,

> *"Greetings (rejoice)! Consider it wholly joyful, my brethren, whenever you are enveloped in or encounter trials of any sort or fall into various temptations. Be assured and understand that the trial and proving of your faith bring out endurance and steadfastness and patience. But let endurance and steadfastness and patience have full play and do a thorough work, so that you may be (people) perfectly and fully developed (with no defects), lacking in nothing. If any of you is deficient in wisdom, let him ask of the giving God (Who gives) to everyone liberally and ungrudgingly, without reproaching or faultfinding, and it will be given him. Only it must be in faith that he asks with no wavering (no hesitating, no doubting), For the one who wavers (hesitates, doubts) is like the billowing surge out at sea that is blown hither and thither and tossed by the wind. For truly, let not such a person imagine that he will receive anything (he asks for) from the Lord. (For being as he is) a man of two minds, (hesitating, dubious, irresolute), (he is) unstable and unreliable and uncertain about everything (he thinks, feels, and decides). Let the brother in humble circumstances glory in his elevation (as a Christian, called to the true riches and be an heir of God).*

And the rich (person ought to glory) in being humbled (by being shown his human frailty) because like the flower of the grass he will pass away. For the sun comes up with a scorching heat and parches the grass; its flower falls off and its beauty fades away. Even so will the rich man wither and die in the midst of his pursuits. Blessed (happy, to be envied) is the man who is patient under trial and stands up under temptation, for when he has stood the test and been approved, he will receive (the victor's) crown of life which God has promised to those who love Him. (James 1:1–12 AMP)

Introduction

When my husband, Jerry, and my best friend, Connie Harris's husband, Lee, died 33 days apart in the fall of 2001, we discovered we didn't have a personal theology for suffering or trials—things hard to deal with and hard to bear. In our quest for answers to our own pain we discovered the church of today as a whole really didn't have a good theology for suffering either. Much could be found about avoidance of suffering, but we found ourselves in the position of having to endure.

What we have found to be reality is that all of us experience things that are hard to deal with and hard to bear. But fearing rejection, judgment, and criticism from our peers in the faith we stifle the pain in our hearts pretending all is well. If the circumstance becomes public, and we can't deny we are in a difficult place causing suffering in our lives, our answer has been to change churches or move geographically for a fresh start where no one knows us to avoid embarrassment, ridicule, and condemnation. Needless to say, we don't come through the rough, dark places of life very successfully and most of the time we don't grow through the process.

I have been an associate pastor of a large church since 1991, and Connie and Lee Harris have attended there since moving to the community in 1997. God wouldn't let us change churches or move, even though we wanted to desperately. We had to walk out the loss of our husbands, not getting our prayers answered for their miraculous recoveries in front of everyone we knew. It is much easier to stay in faith when you get your miracle than to stay in faith when you don't. Even though we wanted to run, today we are very glad God kept us under His hand, immovable in the midst of the darkest, hardest, season of our lives.

The lack of an articulated suffering theology in the church today is keeping us in the shallowness of our personal wildernesses like the children of Israel. They didn't think there should be any suffering either, and if God tested their surrender to Him by withholding necessary elements of living, they revealed how deep their reliance, surrender, and trust was in God.

The enemy wants to keep us hidden from one another in our suffering. When there is suffering our reaction is, "There must be something wrong with me that I am struggling like this." We see everyone else looking good in the faith, while we feel like we are going down for the third time. Quite frankly those not suffering are also asking the question, "What have they done to be suffering like that?" The general rule is that suffering or things hard to deal with or hard to bear are equated with punishment or inadequate faith so we pretend we aren't dealing with anything to not be associated with punishment or a lack of faith.

The truth is in the midst of hard places, things that are hard to deal with and hard to bear, we find gateways into a deeper personal surrender and worship to God. Suffering isn't to punish us; it is to perfect us. Except for the grace of God, all of us deserve punishment. Our paradigm of suffering has caused us to remain shallow, immature children of God tossed to and fro by every gust of adversity. Suffering is to perfect us into instruments of peace held in the grip of God's grace immovable and unshakable, mature in character, endurance, and patience. We must begin to understand God's perfecting process.

I have titled this book "The Crawl Space" in reference to the dark, ugly, shallow space beneath a house containing all the behind the scenes support system for living in the house. Events of life sometimes seem to drop us into dark, ugly, constricting circumstances resembling a "crawl space." If you are in a "crawl space" in the midst of pressure or a dark season of your life that is hard to deal with and hard to bear, this book will change your paradigm as to why you are there and what it is to produce in your life. If you have been in a "crawl space" and have successfully come through it to greater glory, this book with help you articulate what you have discovered to others who don't understand. If you were in a "crawl space" but aborted the process, this book will give you insight for the next time you are faced with a "crawl space" experience as to how to grow in the midst of the difficulty from faith to faith, grace to grace, and glory to glory.

What we discovered in our journey of suffering gave us strength and hope of a new day. There is a sound, original with you, that God wants to bring forth. It is unlike anything else. It is your destiny and purpose for being on this earth. God will never develop your destiny without adversity. If you are in the darkness of adversity, worship! Your relationship with God the Father, God the Son, and God the Holy Spirit is about plunge to a new and glorious depth of intimacy that you have never experienced before, and your destiny is soon to be revealed.

1
Help Me! I'm Stuck in the Crawl Space!

Several years ago, while living in a 900 square foot house with our four year old son, Nathan, toddling at our feet my husband, Jerry, and I discovered we were expecting our second child. We had to have a larger house. Our options were move or add on to the home where we were living. We decided to add on. The addition we planned, gained us another bedroom, bath, and dining room. We worked continuously to finish the new addition before the birth of our new baby. By the time nine months had passed, we were in the final stages of pregnancy and new construction. Saturday, the twelfth day of July of 1986, Jerry and I were plumbing the new bathroom.

We did everything together, so with much difficulty I descended into the crawl space. We lived in rural, south central Kansas, and houses there were either built over basements or a much shorter unfinished version known as the crawl space. In the crawl space, you'll find all the behind the scenes function of the house. The crawl space contains plumbing, electrical, heating and cooling air ducts, cobwebs, dirt, and odds and ends left over from projects of yesteryear (after all it is just the crawl space—who needs to pick up after themselves in an area that is NEVER seen by the public?) Houses in other areas of the country are built on slabs of concrete—not ours. Over the 19 years we lived in that particular old house, we became very familiar with the crawl space.

To access the crawl space in our new addition, we cut a hole in the floor that was only as wide as the 16 inch centered

The Crawl Space

floor joists would allow in a closet where no one would see. Of course, most of the time the hole was covered by a piece of plywood covered with the closet carpet to hide the fact there was a hole. I fit okay from side to side between the 16 inch-centered floor joists, but my nine-month baby overhang barely made it through the 22 inches from front to back. Of course, the access hole was the full length of the 36-foot addition away from the new bathroom facilities.

Crawl spaces are just that—crawl spaces. On all fours we crawled from one end to the other of that dark cavern illuminated with a trouble light. Maternity clothes in those days were generally loose fitting, and the top I was wearing was continually getting under my knees as I crawled. My lightning fast mind—after many times of not being able to move forward and nearly colliding face first with the dirt—decided to tuck my top into my lovely pair of spandex pants.

Jerry was ahead with the light, and I was bringing up the rear—literally, when something extremely furry crossed the back of my leg. In a flash of time my thoughts suddenly became verbal, "SKUNK!" Wham! My head tried to create another access hole. I discovered our cat had found the open hole and had come to join us, but not before my declaration of "SKUNK" had set off a chain reaction so Jerry's head didn't feel too good either. I don't know where we thought we would go or how we thought we would have been able to get there (wherever "there" was) very fast if it were a skunk, but we were certainly moving fast on the inside.

Regaining our composure (if composure is actually the right word for a crawl space) Jerry and I dragged everything needed for the job from one end of the addition to the other. We measured and fitted pipes for both hot and cold water to all the bathroom fixtures and the big four-inch sewer drain out. Since this was a new addition, we had to cut a hole in the foundation of the old house to allow the new water lines access into the new addition. Because of our terrific preplanning, the hole for all the water lines came directly under the access hole to the crawl space. The four-inch sewer line had to come directly under the access hole since that was the most direct route to the main sewer drain.

This had been an all day job. I had been able to get out of the crawl space hole as needed from time to time during the day by my own strength. Then we made the last few connections. All the while we were connecting pipes under the access hole it never once occurred to us that the final pipe connections might be in the way for me to get back out.

We finished the plumbing under the house and we were ready to make our ascent when, Jerry, being the gentleman he was, wanted me to get out first. That was when we discovered all the pipes we had labored so hard to put in that day were in the way of my being able to get out. Try as I might, I could not get through the hole. I felt like a round peg trying to fit through a square hole. At nine months pregnant I certainly could not be accused of agility, so twisting in contortionist shapes to prevent standing on freshly cemented pipes was completely out of the question. I was so heavy, I didn't have enough strength to lift myself out without using my legs, and when I tried to pull myself out, I seemed to get even bulkier if *that* was possible.

Jerry was ready to cut the pipes. All he could see was having a baby in the crawl space. He knew I had been getting out okay before we finished the last connections, so he wanted to cut out a section of pipes to give me an escape route. I am a task-oriented person, and when something gets done, I want it to stay that way. We had worked too hard to complete the project and I was too close to due date to have to make repairs to new pipes. I certainly did not want to cut the pipes. Jerry and I sat down in the dirt in the crawl space under the house illuminated by only a trouble light (what a fitting name) covered with dirt from head to toe and stared at each other. Suddenly we had an idea. If Jerry would get out of the crawl space and I would stretch my hands up to him through the hole, *maybe* he would be able to pull me through with no assistance from me. It was certainly worth a try.

Jerry climbed out and stood directly over the hole. I got as close to the hole as I could with my back to the pipes, lifted my hands, and the pull began. He pulled so slowly, I began to question if he really had the strength to pull me out. I was so heavy with child and without being able to put forth any effort of my own to help him, thoughts of "What if he drops me?" surfaced. I was totally in a position that all I could do was trust him completely with our unborn child and all of me.

Jerry pulled so slowly to prevent hurting me or our baby, but by this time the hole had gotten smaller, the crawl space seemed even darker, and I was huge in my thinking. Feeling very confined and claustrophobic I just wanted out. A good, hard, fast yank would have been all right with me, but Jerry continued to pull ever so slowly until he had pulled me completely out of the crawl space and sat me on the floor. Finally, with cobwebs stringing from my bedraggled hair, my top still tucked into my spandex pants in the front, and covered from head to toe with dirt, I was sitting on the floor a sight for sore eyes, gratefully free of the crawl space, and more in love with my husband than ever. Despite my "Dillard's" appearance—NOT!—Jerry was more in love with me than ever. Through the process, I had gained a new respect and admiration for my strong, wonderful husband who had safely pulled me through while keeping the pipes intact.

Why am I telling you this story? Events of life will drop us into "crawl spaces." My best friend and co-founder with me of Walk With Me Ministries, Connie Harris, and I were dropped into a crawl space of life in the fall of 2001. Connie's husband, Lee, and my husband, Jerry, died 33 days apart in the months of September and October. We tell our story in our book entitled "No Time For Goodbyes" (Tate Publishing, LLC.). Suffice it to say in this writing that the untimely death of our husbands in their mid-forties dropped us into darkest days of our lives where at first we didn't even seem to have a trouble light.

It is staggering to think about all the changes that have occurred in our lives since the deaths of our husbands. Our families are forever changed. We are not the same inwardly as we were prior to their deaths. In thinking about all the changes, it occurred to me how similar the changes happening in our lives were like the natural changes of the seasons. Even as the season of summer looks nothing like winter yet it is the same world, so our lives are nothing like they were before the death of our husbands yet we are still the same people. A crawl space experience is essentially a period of transition that will ultimately change the season of our life. Natural seasons are necessary for growth in the physical world. It follows that changing seasons are necessary for growth in our inner man as well.

2
Seasons Change In Crawl Spaces

Matthew 7:13–14 says, *"Enter through the narrow gate, for wide is the gate and spacious and broad is the way that leads away to destruction, and many are those who are entering through it. But the gate is narrow (contracted by pressure) and the way is straitened and compressed that leads away to life, and few are those who find it."* A crawl space in a home is a constricted, dark, dirty area under the floor of the house where you will find the behind the scenes, internal workings of the house. The crawl space of a house is usually accessed by a very small hole. We never go into the crawl space unless some kind of change is needed to support the life within the house. Even as there are natural crawl spaces there are spiritual crawl spaces. Spiritual crawl spaces contain the internal workings of the heart of man—the character, integrity, patience, endurance, steadfastness, and the deep processing of intimacy with our Father God.

We live our lives within the demarcation of time. We recognize minutes, moments, hours, days, weeks, months, and years, but we seldom have recognized the seasons of our lives. We live life in seasons. Generally speaking, we have little understanding of the real purpose of "crawl space" experiences but they are the gateway to *"counting everything as loss compared to the possession of the priceless privilege of knowing Christ Jesus my Lord and of progressively becoming more deeply and intimately acquainted with Him. For His sake I have lost everything and consider it all to be mere rubbish in order that I may win Christ . . . not having any (self-achieved) righteousness that can be called my own . . . and, that I may so share His sufferings as to be continually transformed (in spirit into His likeness even) to His death, (in the hope) that if possible I may attain to the (spiritual and moral) resurrection (that lifts me) out from among the dead (even while in the body) . . ."* (Philippians 3:8–16 AMP) Many times major changes of the seasons of life come in the midst of a crawl space experience.

The language we hear the most and has the most impact on our lives isn't the language we hear with our ears; it is the language of our circumstances. Circumstances that drop us into crawl spaces give us the opportunity of moving past the shallowness of our understanding of who God is that we have heard with our ears to the experiential understanding of who God is in the depth of our hearts. We can choose to go deep into His presence progressively becoming more deeply and intimately acquainted with Him described in Philippians three, or we can stay in the shallowness of our human understanding and way of living only knowing a God we have heard about.

What comes naturally to us to do in the midst of a crawl space is manipulate our circumstances however we see fit to get out of the crawl space as quickly as possible declaring our faith has seen us through. If our faith has seen us through, then it should follow that we can also say our character has matured to a new level. We are walking in a keener sense of integrity, and we have found a deeper surrender of our right to our self and our will to His will and purpose. We will also discover more of His grace is being revealed through our life and we have a more intimate personal relationship with Him. Instead, most of the time all we can say is "I got what I wanted." Every event surrendered to God in worship trusting Him to bring us through without our manipulation or "cutting the pipes" has the potential of moving us from grace to grace, faith to faith, and glory to glory.

Development Happens in the Dark

I am reminded of a picture I saw in my spirit some time ago. There were a multitude of people snorkeling on top of the ocean splashing around to their hearts content seeing what they could see from the top of the water. There were a few who weren't content with seeing and knowing only from the shallowness of the surface. They were diving deep into the dark waters and discovering the deep hidden secrets that could not be seen from the surface. These hidden secrets were becoming such a part of who they were, and the knowledge they were acquiring was changing them to be completely different from the surface "snorkelers.'" There was a calm, peaceful, grace about their movements and responses as they moved about in the depths below the surface. The sound produced by those who snorkeled on the surface describing what they had seen could not compare to the treasures brought up from the depths by those not content with surface swimming.

> **When it comes time for the destiny to be revealed in our own lives we most likely will go through a period of darkness brought to us through the language of our circumstances.**

Isaiah 45:3 says, *"I will give you treasures of darkness and hidden riches of secret places that you may know that it is I, the Lord, the God of Israel, Who calls you by your name."* It is in the dark places God develops us. God never develops us in the light. We will never be developed apart from adversity. It is in the crawl spaces, the places that are hard to deal with and hard to bear, that God develops us. Film isn't developed in the light. It is developed in the dark, and then the picture of what has been developed is brought to the light for all to see. Even a baby is developed in the darkness of the confinement of his mother's womb and in the fullness of time is brought out into the light. When it comes time for the destiny to be revealed in our own lives we most likely will go through a period of darkness brought to us through the language of our circumstances.

Life happens to all of us. Some of life is good, and quite frankly, some of the facts of life stink. Ecclesiastes 3:1–8 tells of the cycle of life. *"To everything there is a season, and a time for every matter or purpose under heaven: A time to be born and a time to die, a time to plant and a time to pluck up what is planted, a time to kill and a time to heal, a time to break down and time to build up, a time to weep and a time to laugh, a time to mourn and time to dance, a time to cast away stones and a time to gather stones together, a time to embrace and a time to refrain from embracing, a time to get and a time to lose, at time to keep and a time to cast away, a time to rend and a time to sew, a time to keep silence and a time to speak, a time to love and time to hate, a time for war and a time for peace."* We have defined half of this passage of scripture as "bad things" and the other half "good things" when the wisest man who ever lived and who also authored this book, Solomon, goes on to say in verse 11, *"God has made everything beautiful in its time."*

We don't see the purpose or the beauty in what we define as being the "ugly" part, or the dark crawl spaces of life, but the very seasons of nature—winter, summer, fall, and spring—show us there is a time to produce foliage and fruit (the seen) and then there is a time to work on the root (the unseen). Springtime and summer produce beautiful green foliage and fruit yielding harvest. Yet in nature it does not surprise us when winter comes, the foliage dies, and the fruit is gone. We understand in the season of winter and harsh conditions the root of the plant, or tree becomes stronger and goes deeper. We then know spring is coming with new foliage and fruit in greater measure than the year prior. We don't view winter as punishing the tree, but perfecting it, making it stronger and more enduring capable of producing more fruit. Even though all looks dead, we know not to dig up the tree or vegetation. We wait patiently for spring to come. Seasons change in our lives also, not to punish us but to perfect us.

Seasons change in our lives also, not to punish us but to perfect us.

Life has become an idol to us. If we are beautiful, full of fruit, lots of prosperity, and all looks good, then all is well, but let a season of winter come whose sole purpose is to cause our roots to go deeper developing the unseen to be totally dependent on the Giver of Life, and we abort. "Cut the pipes! Let me out of here!" For natural life to be healthy there has to be a balance between root and fruit, or another way of saying it is there has to be a balance between the internal and the external. There is a time for growth to strengthen and establish the roots or the unseen part, and then there is a time to produce fruit. A plant can become root bound producing no fruit or it can have such a small root system it can't support a healthy life. Likewise, to have a healthy spirit being—we are spirit, have a soul, and live in a body—there has to be a time of concentrated root or spirit growth as well as fruit production.

The root or the spirit is the center of our being. Ecclesiastes 3:11 says, *"He also has planted eternity in men's hearts and minds* (a divinely implanted sense of purpose working through the ages which nothing under the sun but God alone can satisfy), *yet so that men cannot find out what God has done from the beginning to the end."* God has planted within each of us a sense of purpose and destiny that God alone can satisfy. Our self-centeredness is at war against our divine purpose to choke it out. The crawl spaces of life are the opportunities for God to expose and bring death to our self-centeredness releasing the seed of destiny in our lives. The war is over which will win—the seed of destiny or self-centeredness.

Sadly, most of the time in a crawl space, all we see is the dark and the dirt and how we are affected and offended by it. We want out of the dark and the dirt as fast as possible, and we will go to great lengths to make it happen because we want to be comfortable not constricted. We experience lack in the midst of dark times, and we don't like to feel lack. Surely nothing good can come from bad situations. The truth is bad situations, crawl spaces, things that are hard to deal with and hard to bear is where God—if we allow Him the opportunity—can begin to develop the seed of destiny that He has put within us. There is a seed of greatness that God has placed within each one of us. Many of us never find that seed because we are too focused on ourselves, the dirt, and the hard place we have been thrown into. Instead of surrendering ourselves to the Father in worship in the midst of the crawl space allowing Him the opportunity to bring forth the seed of destiny or the treasures and hidden secrets from the darkness in our lives, we are looking for a way out.

Don't Cut the Pipes

If you will remember, Jerry wanted to cut the pipes in my pregnant crawl space experience. He knew if he cut the pipes, I could get out. Many times when we are in the crawl spaces of life, we find our own way out by cutting the pipes, and we abort the whole process of what God wants to bring forth in our lives. In "cutting the pipes" we are trying to fill the lack we feel by our own means. Anytime we take it upon ourselves to fill a need or fix a problem, we are heading down a road of unrighteousness. We never sin to make more problems for ourselves. We sin to try to fix a problem or fill a felt need. Instead of trusting God to make us complete in the area of the felt need, we fill that need by our own way of thinking. If our solution doesn't line up with what the Word says, which is God's ascribed righteousness, then we have sinned and have become disobedient to God. We will find ourselves in repeated crawl spaces of the same nature. God, in His patient dealing with us, makes every opportunity for us to pass the test and surrender those areas of our lives to Him in order to make us complete. It takes the grace of God to stay under the hand of God in the midst of a crawl space experience, but that is the only way the destiny that God has put within us will be revealed.

I was *very* pregnant in the crawl space. Our son, Brian Alan, was born 33 hours after Jerry pulled me out of that hole. If you will stay in the crawl space, under the hand of God, allowing God to bring you out, He will produce new resurrected life by the power of God through you when you come to the light. Jerry and I were so busy with new construction, we had not decided on a name for Brian. We took him home from the hospital without a name much to hospital record's dismay. He was called "Baby Boy

Sidebottom." We didn't know what to name him, and we weren't going to be rushed. Many times when God brings you out of a crawl space experience you don't know what to call what God has done in you and is birthing through you. All you know is that it is a "Holy Thing" and God has done it. You know He is calling you by your name.

Many things can send us to the crawl space: death (especially if we feel like it was premature), bad marriage, divorce, wayward children, bankruptcy, etc., all requiring change. We never go into the crawl space of a house unless there is a need for change. The crawl space is where we go through our metamorphosis. If we don't abort the process and find our own way out, God uses the difficult events of life to develop the destiny and purpose within us. That is where He develops His character within us. He removes our self-centeredness and fills us with Himself. It is in the darkness that we truly discover the hidden riches of secret places and treasures that are then brought out into the light to be revealed to those in the house. Yes, the enemy meant "it" for evil to destroy us, but surrendered to the hand of God it will turn out for our good.

If we abort the process, we may find ourselves time after time in more crawl space experiences. If Jerry and I would have aborted the process and cut the pipes, we would have found ourselves back down in the dark place, working again on the same thing until the integrity of the line was established to support the new bathroom. The same goes for the crawl spaces of life. If we abort and find our own way out, we may find ourselves in the dark again and again. God is very patient and kind. He will give every opportunity for the seed of destiny to be revealed in us. Our challenge is seeing past the tight, dirty crawl space to discover the seed. Without a vision of the seed of destiny within us, we will abort the seed. None of us enjoy being in tight difficult places. Our flesh wants to find the way out of least resistance, but the seed of destiny will only be developed through adversity so that we may know it is God who has called us by our name.

If we can gain a new understanding of what the crawl

space of life is all about, maybe we will have fewer "abortions" in the midst of the confusion of the darkness—possibly only illuminated by a trouble light—and a greater number of new "births" as we exit our crawl space experiences dependent upon the Father God. As in my natural crawl space experience with my husband, Jerry, the only way we will exit the crawl spaces of life—successfully birthing the seed of destiny within us—is to discover our total dependence upon our Father God by surrendering our selves to Him in the midst of the dark. Even as I gained a new confidence and trust in my husband's ability—having pulled me out of the hole—we gain a *confident surrender, a personal trust, and a firm reliance* on our Father God when He brings us out.

3
Discovering Integrity In The Crawl Space

Because the house I described in the first chapter was built in the late 1800's, Jerry and I have had to access the crawl space of our house for many different reasons—sometimes to correct an existing problem and sometimes to install something new to support the new vision in the house. Quite frankly it really doesn't matter why you have to access the crawl space of the house. It is simply important that all the fundamental basics of living under the house, whether new or old, are functioning properly to support the living in the house. Over time many things can occur that need to be corrected in the crawl space. If the corrections are not taken care of, it can affect our comfort within the house. Pipes can bust, joints can leak, become corroded, or clogged, and foundations can settle and crack. Without regular maintenance or paying attention to details, even a new house can become old very quickly.

Jerry and I have experienced all of the above as young newly weds buying our first home. Both sets of parents told us, "Don't pay rent. You're just pouring money down a rat hole." Of course this is very true, but what we didn't know by virtue of our dads always taking care of everything, was being our own landlord caused the buck to stop with us. Being young and just starting out, all we could afford was an old 900 square foot house, two bedrooms, kitchen, living/dining room combined and one bathroom. I think you could call it a bathroom. It had all the fixtures, but it was so small you had to step out to change your mind. However, I *am* very grateful it *was* indoors.

Being the do-it-yourselfers that we were, when something would go wrong with the house, we would tackle the project. I

The Crawl Space

would like to tell you it was because of the sense of accomplishment of the hope that was set before us, but in truth it was because we were poor as church mice and couldn't afford to hire anything done. We bought books and asked tons of questions. It is amazing how people love to tell you what they know if you ask a specific question, but if you ask them to be your teacher or mentor, they reply, "Oh, I couldn't do that; I wouldn't know the first thing about being a mentor." Thankfully, we found the people we needed to tell us what they knew about the things we needed to do. Then we had to go to the crawl space and apply what we were told or what we had read in a book. Because the house was so old, we began finding problems almost immediately.

Our little bathroom developed a little trickle. Now I for one like a full stream of good water pressure if I am trying to take an invigorating shower. Somehow a trickle doesn't seem to do the job. We discovered the galvanized pipes under the house had become so corroded over time with rust deposits that what should have been carrying a full 3/4 inch stream of water was now reduced to less than a #2 pencil lead. We found ourselves having to replace all of the plumbing under the house. We installed new plastic pipe and all looked wonderful. Jerry exited the crawl space to turn on the water main, while I stayed in the crawl space to be sure of "no leaks, no runs, no errors." The water came back on. I could hear it gurgling in the new pipe. All looked great until the incoming water pressure hit a joint we had failed to glue. What a mess! Instantly I was yelling at the top of my lungs, "TURN IT OFF!" while crawling on all fours in fresh mud, quickly becoming soaked to the skin. Just in case he didn't hear me the first time, I continued screaming over and over, "TURN IT OFF! TURN IT OFF!" In the length of time it took Jerry to get to the house, hear me screaming, and get back to the water main in front of the house to turn the water off, I was sitting in a cold water pond. Needless to say, my husband and I have experienced our share of faulty plumbing. But not to worry, our experiences were not in vain. God gives us the natural to better understand the spiritual.

Fitly Joined Together

Several years ago I began to understand we are only a vessel or pipeline through which the love of God flows like water. We are connected together resembling a network of pipes to allow the refreshing water of the love of God to reach the ends of the earth.

Just as the network of pipes fitly joined together beneath our houses reach the end of each faucet providing fresh life-giving water, we also have this God-given desire to be fitly joined with others to allow the life-giving water of the love and the word of God to flow through our lives to another. God uses those we are connected to as divine influences to move us out of our self-centeredness into Christ-likeness. But, sometimes our relationships with the people to which we are fitly joined develop leaks or even blow apart when the pressure is on. Integrity is the "glue" that holds our relationships together. A lack of integrity in relationships can usually be identified as the root of all "leaky joints" and corrosion, which is ultimately the cause of breakups in relationships.

The love of God flowing through us to others will produce pressure on every joint of relationship, even as incoming fresh water produces pressure in the lines of a house. If there is no pressure in our relationships, they aren't life-giving. When the life-giving water of the word and the love of God begin to flow through our relationships, it will reveal where there is a lack of integrity. We may not like what we see in us as we relate to others, and we may blame what we see in us on the other person, but that life-giving water pressure is how God matures his body. It is also what we fight the most.

> **Integrity is the "glue" that holds our relationships together.**

We may say, "If my spouse, co-worker, boss, children, etc. just wouldn't do 'that,' (whatever 'that' is) I would not get angry or respond the way I do. They need to change." Sometimes Christians even say that they would rather do business with a sinner because then if the sinner doesn't do it the way they think the job ought to be done, they can get mad if they want to. If that is how we think, we know our lack of patience and anger is not revealing the character and integrity of Christ. We don't want to show our sinful attitude to a brother or sister in Christ, but we are willing to hang a heathen for messing up. I remember when the Holy Spirit spoke in my heart, "Sharolyn, your anger is not promoting my righteousness." OUCH! Then of all things I found chapter and verse. James 1:20 states, *"For man's anger does not promote the righteousness God* (wishes and requires)." We may think we are surrounded by incompetent people when God is just setting us up to bring out the worst in us, so we can give it to God and allow His grace to change us into His image. It is only by His grace and ability that we are able to change.

What God is revealing in the midst of our earthly relationships is our individuality then He presses it to the limit to get at our personal life, personality, or personal surrender to Him so our real life with Christ can emerge, grow, and mature. As long as we assert our individualism and our independence, we remain isolated, separated, and out of intimate fellowship with our earthly relationships as well as with God. Individualism acts like a child claiming their own rights. When we do this we are reduced to the small package of self. Until the hardness of our individualism (characteristic of our natural man) is broken away, our real personality (characteristic of our Spiritual man) cannot emerge. We must be willing to give up our right to our individualism or self-centeredness in order for our personality (that which is original with us) to be revealed. Faith is leaning our entire personality (who we really are without being hidden behind a shell of individualism) on the Father. When we begin to merge our personality with another is when we discover our real identity.

So many say, "I have to find myself and I don't know whether that includes 'you' (meaning the current relationship) or not." What we don't understand is to find our "self" means to find our personality, which is hidden under our individuality. We mistake finding ourselves for living in our individualism apart from anyone else. The pressure we feel on our individualism in the midst of a relationship is exactly what God is using to get at our real life to bring us into intimate union with Him and His body. He wants to shatter our individualism so that the light of our personality will shine through. There is so much more to us than the external shell of our individualism. When we lose our individualism is when we find our real selves.

We think if we are in love life should always be pleasant, soft, and kind, filled with romantic moments, but relationships that never produce pressure will never cause growth in our lives. It is amazing how opposite personalities attract. Opposite personalities see everything from a different perspective. Once you throw gender differences plus environmental differences of childhood development into the mix, you have instituted an atmosphere for pressure points to occur. God designed it this way to grow us up into His character, integrity, and likeness. As children we tend to be catered to as our physical growth occurs. Then as young adults we develop a sense of individualism and we think we know who we are and that everything is all about us. But when we begin to become one with another, the deep processing of who we really are actually begins to occur, and the pressure placed by intimate living with another begins to cause attitudes of the heart to surface we did not even know were there.

Don't Play in the Sewer

Pressure is not our problem. Lack of integrity is our problem. Integrity is the glue that joins us and keeps us together. The new plastic pipe Jerry and I replaced the galvanized pipe with under our house was all cut to fit. Although it looked like all the connections were in place, when the pressure of the incoming water hit the joint that had not been glued properly, it blew apart. Our relationships can look good on the outside, but if we are not walking in integrity with one another, they will eventually blow apart. A truly God-given relationship will bring out the very best and the very worst in us. Depending on how we deal with the very worst that surfaces determines whether the relationship will stay together. Webster's dictionary defines integrity as: "Incorruptibility: An unimpaired condition: Soundness: The quality or state of being complete or undivided: Completeness: Honesty." If we allow corruption of any kind to come into our relationships, it will destroy the soundness of the relationship. Allowing offenses or walking dishonestly with one another will begin to divide and destroy.

We've not been good at dealing with the worst. Dealing with the worst makes me have to deal with who I am. It is so much easier to say, "I am the way and I am. You deal with it. It's your fault I respond the way I do. You bring out the worst in me." Yes, "they" do. That is how God gets at the very worst in us. Instead of blaming the other person, our response should be to cry out for God's grace to change the worst in us and mature us in the area where pressure has revealed the lack of integrity in our own character.

Water lines bearing no pressure are for sewage. The drain or sewage lines of a house all go down hill taking the way of least resistance. They are simply to remove the used fresh water away from the premises never to be seen again. Fresh water with a certain amount of scrubbing and force, removes dirt and germs carried away by the drain line. Similarly, the pressure of being connected to another person reveals the "dirt and germs" in our character that need to be washed away by the love and the grace of God. Pressure must come before the "sewage" of our character can be revealed and removed. Our relationships with people produce that pressure. If the purpose of the pressure from being joined to another is understood and we stop blaming the other person for our reactions to pressure, it has the potential of allowing the grace of God to change us, remove the sewage from our character, and mature His character within us. If you find a relationship you think is wonderful without the stress of the current relationship you are in, it's a trick. You will soon find yourself playing in the sewer no longer walking uprightly before God.

Any relationship no matter how good it is has to be walked out in dependency upon the grace of God if it is going to stay together. When we bump into disturbances, opposition, or difficulties we begin to think this relationship must not be of God when most likely it is. Disturbances give opportunity for God to become greater in our eyes than our spouse, our friends or other family members, even as He was greater in David's eyes than Goliath. Our relationship challenges aren't an end but a gateway through which you can experience a greater intimacy and knowledge of the love of God and who He is than ever before. David didn't see Goliath as an end but a gateway into Kingdom living receiving all Saul promised to the one who would defeat Goliath. Our challenges can also be a gateway into Kingdom living understanding God's methods and ways of doing and being. David didn't defeat Goliath by anything he could do but by leaning or surrendering all of who he was into his covenant with God almighty. Our "Goliaths" will be defeated the same way.

Let's be careful that we don't fall prey to a spirit of lack, thinking, "My spouse isn't meeting my needs." It's a trick! No spouse can meet our needs. Our true needs go much deeper than the physical. Our true need is to be devoted to the person of Jesus Christ. When we begin to feel our spouse isn't meeting our needs we have not been pressing into the presence of God. Only God can meet our needs and make us a complete person. If we are looking for our spouse or anyone else to meet our needs, we will soon be drinking stolen waters from someone else's well, justifying our adultery and seeking God's forgiveness.

An attitude has crept into our thinking that it is easier, and in some situations, better to sin and then get forgiveness than to never sin at all. This attitude is based out of self-centeredness motivated by the desires of our flesh. Thinking this way we can have what we want and get forgiveness too. After all, it is easier to get forgiveness than permission isn't it? But, faith is the personal surrender of our will to the Father God regardless of the circumstance. What have we truly surrendered in a sin/forgive mindset? All we are surrendering is an unrighteous act asking God to forgive us of what we have done rather than surrendering the root of our action—our will—before we act. God wants our personal surrender to Him to allow Him by His grace to deliver us from our self-centeredness into His righteousness. It is much better to live surrendered to His will, walking in His grace, power, and ability than to be continually living in need of His mercy.

Love covers a multitude of sin in that while we were yet sinners Christ died for us. In His sinless life, death, burial, resurrection, and ascension to the right hand of the Father He gave us grace, God's power and ability, to deliver us from being dominated and controlled by sin. Mercy will forgive us of our willful disobedience but we tend to forget actions produce consequences. Consequences can deal a heavy blow. We then begin believing God for mercy to remove the consequences we find ourselves in. If we truly believe we have the faith to remove the consequences after we have sinned, when at that point the enemy is making us feel like a filthy heel, wouldn't it be better to believe God for His grace to prevent us from sinning in the first place. It is one thing to endure consequences for our own actions, but we take little thought for how our actions will affect our children.

What About Our Children

The enemy doesn't even mind if God forgives us. He wants the ability to continue to plague our future generations with the same deceit in the hopes of eternal destruction in their lives. With our sin he has gained an entrance to haunt our lineage with covenant breaking, adultery, sexual immorality, and whatever else is allowed entrance for generations to come—to the third and fourth generation. (Exodus 20:5) Perhaps we know enough in our generation to seek forgiveness. But, will our future generations have the same cry in their heart for forgiveness, or will the seed of sin sown with us in our generation come to complete maturity in our children and grandchildren causing eternal death in them?

The devil has been around a long time. He can out wait us. Each generation has a different paradigm and mental processing than the last. Our values will not necessarily be our posterity's values. We can see that by looking back to the values and the paradigms we knew our parents to have and realizing how different we are from them. As an example my parents raised me on the old hymns of the faith but my children have been raised during the last 20 years of contemporary worship. They know very few hymns by virtue of the shift in congregational worship. Whether that is good or bad is not the point. The point is what we know may not be what our children will know in future generations, but the weakness stamped in their spiritual DNA because of our sin will be certain to pass from generation to generation as the familial spirit seeks new dwelling places until someone breaks the iniquitous sin pattern by the blood of Jesus and removes the enemy's hook from the lineage. Sometimes we have to go through a crawl space to do it.

It's not all about us and what we want. We may get what we want for the moment in this lifetime. It may feel good for a while, but is it worth allowing the hook of the enemy into our families? Our unrighteous act in the flesh is nothing in comparison to the seed sown in the heavenlies against our posterity because of it. Which of our children and how many are we willing to sacrifice on the altar of our self-centeredness? We say, "Mess with me, but don't mess with my children!" We don't realize our sin behavior is allowing the enemy to mess with our children to a much greater degree than any human being could ever mess with them on this earth. We are giving the enemy opportunity to mess with their eternity.

In reading these words, if the Holy Spirit has convicted your heart of where sin was allowed to gain entrance into your family through you or your ancestry, cry out for the grace of God to cleanse and deliver your family from sin's dominion. Choose this day to turn from unrighteousness, and by the grace of God, speak the blood of Jesus against the spiritual weakness that has been allowed to enter your family's DNA. Stop it from traveling to future generations.

Spiritual DNA

Even as we have a physical DNA, we have a spiritual DNA. Doctors take our physical history to understand physical weaknesses that could be found in the present and future generations; likewise spiritual weakness where sin has gained access travel from generation to generation. Every family lineage has a God-given destiny. The enemy does his best to thwart the purpose of God in each family. If he can't stop it in our generation, he at least wants a hook in the family so he can stop the destiny placed by God in a family lineage in future generations. This holds true for our ancestry. Many times the God given destiny of our ancestral generations was stopped because of sin and the enemy getting a hook in them. In that case maybe you are the one who will rise up by the grace of God and the blood of Jesus and render the sin that has plagued your family for generations powerless, delivering your family back into its God-given destiny and purpose for being on this earth. I wonder what kind of revelation of the glory of God would take place on the earth if we would begin to cry out to God to fulfill the God-given destiny intended for our family in us.

Covenant Relationships

The enemy is after covenant relationships. He wants them broken to prevent the multiplied power of God from operating in the earth. A covenant relationship means two people coming together as one spiritually, emotionally, and mentally. The enemy hates that because in becoming one, there is a mutual laying down of our lives to the other—our ideas, desires, and goals for the other, beginning a journey of spiritual discovery of who God is together. That brings death to self-centeredness, and that is the only venue the enemy has to work through.

I purposely left out physical union for this reason. If the only reason we are getting into a relationship with someone is because of physical attraction and fulfillment of our physical desires, that isn't covenant. Our purpose for relationship is self-centered. What has begun in self-centeredness will more than likely end in self-centeredness. When the other person stops pleasing you, all the wonderful words of love and commitment that was spoken to the other person will become meaningless and the person is replaced by someone new. Many times the pattern then repeats over and over.

A covenant is made by giving our word. A covenant relationship is sustained by keeping our word by faith regardless, in spite of, no matter what, forever and for always. In the Vine's Expository Dictionary the term "covenant breakers" is synonymous with being "faithless." It takes faith to see beyond the present difficulty of any relationship and stay in covenant believing God to be greater than our disturbance and that His grace will take the frustrations and give us peace.

In Luke 18 Jesus tells the story of the widow and the unjust judge who answered her plea because she wearied him. In verses 7–9 Jesus says, *"Then the Lord said, Listen to what the unjust judge says! And will not* (our just) *God defend and protect and avenge His elect* (His chosen ones), *who cry to Him day and night? Will He defer them and delay help on their behalf? I tell you, He will defend and protect and avenge them speedily. However, when the Son of Man comes, will He find* (persistence in) *faith on the earth? He also told this parable to some people who trusted in themselves and were confident that they were righteous* (that they were upright and in right standing with God) *and scorned and made nothing of all the rest of men."*

The question still remains today. Will He find faith (persistence) when He comes? Will He find people keeping their word, emptied of self, surrendered to Him, trusting Him to "defend, protect, and avenge," or will He only find people who trusted in themselves and what they thought to be the right thing to do throughout their journey of life. The way of least resistance is not persistence. Continually worshiping the Father in the midst of our circumstances keeping our eyes on Him is the only way we will stay faithful, enduring, steadfast, and persistent allowing Him to mature us, developing a grace in our lives that will come no other way.

> **The way of least resistance is not persistence.**

We have made resisting the devil and resisting circumstances synonymous. Our form of resisting the devil has been to say, "I rebuke you devil" or "I bind you devil in the name of Jesus." We have prayed "change my circumstances" and rebuked and bound them also, but to resist something describes action. Resist means to exert oneself in opposition so as to counteract or defeat. We have rebuked and bound but I am not sure we have truly learned how to exert ourselves in opposition to counteract the devil. To exert ourselves in opposition would mean to do the opposite of what is desired. If the devil desires and thrives on our self-centeredness then resisting would be refusing to live in self-centeredness.

Self-Centeredness or Christ-Centeredness

Circumstances are opportunities for God to change us into His image moving us from self-centeredness to Christ-likeness. We have resisted the very thing God was using to bring spiritual maturity in us by truly showing us what to resist. Self-centeredness is what we are to resist in the midst of good or bad circumstances. We have said good is from God and bad is from the devil. The truth is we can live self-centered in the midst of good as well as bad circumstances. Bad circumstances just reveal how self-centered we really are and how much we believe life to be all about us and what we want.

Living life self-centered is the purest form of worship to Satan. Self-centeredness (worshiping Satan) is what we are to resist. We are to resist the temptation of making everything be all about you and what you want. If you won't worship the devil with self-centeredness, he will flee. Why stay where you are not worshiped. Self-centeredness will continue to hold us in the grip of circumstances and I would venture to say most of us have been held in the grip of circumstances.

Christ-centeredness will release us from the grip of circumstances and hold us in the grip of His love and grace. Very few of us have really been held in the grip of God's love unmoved by circumstances. Self-centeredness must be nailed to the cross of

Christ if we are ever going to experience being held in the grip of God's love, continually walking in serene peace free from fear and agitating passions.

Self-centeredness or being focused on our self is the root of all fear and divisions. If we are focused on our self, when bad circumstances happen and we are dropped into a crawl space, we become afraid of how we will be affected. One of the first thoughts to surface in our minds is, "What am I going to do?" Focusing on our self will open the door for fear and panic to set in. Divisions come in relationships when we focus on our self. I want my way. I don't care what you want or how what I want will affect you. I am only interested in how I am affected. Resist the temptation to walk in self-centeredness. Self-centeredness will hold you in a grip of fear, panic, anxiety attacks, bad relationships, family divisions, etc. James 4:4–10 says:

> **Living life self-centered is the purest form of worship to Satan.**

> *"You are like unfaithful wives having illicit love affairs with the world, and breaking your marriage vow to God! Do you not know that being the world's friend is being God's enemy? So whoever chooses to be a friend of the world takes his stand as an enemy of God. Or do you suppose that the Scripture is speaking to no purpose that says, The Spirit Whom He has caused to dwell in us yearns over us and He yearns for the Spirit to be welcome with a jealous love?*

Pursuing what can be gained for ourselves from the world more than pursuing God is spiritual adultery. Self-focus will cause us to explore the world's methods and ways of meeting our needs rather than seeking God and His righteousness. After all, we know God wants us blessed and since He seems to be moving a bit too slow we will just find a "friend" that will move a little faster. No, the Holy Spirit of God wants our undivided attention.

> *"But He gives us more and more grace* (power of the Holy Spirit, to meet this evil tendency and all others fully). *That is why He says, God sets Himself against the proud and haughty but gives grace* (continually) *to the lowly."*

Grace is the power and ability of God Almighty to subdue and conquer every evil tendency. He says He gives us more and more power and ability. This reminds me of the passage, "where sin abounds grace doth much more." Those who are proud and haughty are those who are living self-centered lives believing life is all about "me" and what "I" want, but He gives His power and ability to those who are humbly surrendering their will to the will of the Father seeking His face.

> *"So be subject to God. Resist the devil and he will flee from you. Come close to God and He will come close to you.* (Recognize that you are) *sinners, get your soiled hands clean; wavering individuals with divided interests, and purify your hearts* (of your spiritual adultery). (As you draw near to God) *be deeply penitent and grieve, even weep* (over your disloyalty). *Let your laughter be turned to grief and your mirth to dejection and heartfelt shame* (for your sins)."

Surrender your self and selfishness to God. Resist the temptation to worship the devil with your self-centeredness. He won't stay where he is not worshiped. Focus your attention on God. Recognize that you have been selfish and disloyal, sometimes declaring surrender to the Father and sometimes declaring self-centeredness. Spiritual adultery is loving self more than God. We can tell what we love the most by what we seek the most. If self is the center of our lives we will busy ourselves in achieving our own ambitions and if we have the time and energy left of over we will give attention to our relationship with God. If God is the center our relationship with Him will be the focus of our attention and the rest of our life will bow to Him.

> *"Humble yourselves* (feeling very insignificant) *in the presence of the Lord, and He will exalt you* (He will lift you up and make your lives significant).*"*

A life deemed to be successful by the pride of human effort is not worthy to be compared to the glory of a life made significant by the hand of God.

Significant Things Happen in a Crawl Space

There is a hope to which He has called you and set you apart for. There is a seed of destiny original with you that will declare a new facet of His glory. He will make your life significant. Your circumstances have everything to do with Him developing that precious seed within you so you will be empty of self-centeredness and filled with Himself. It is not what happens to you but what happens in you because of what is happening to you. Let our prayer be "change me to reflect You in the midst of my circumstances. Grace, Father, Grace!" I hope our paradigm is changing to understand it is not about us, but it is all about Him not just in word but in real life application.

Hopefully Ephesians 1:17–19 will take on new meaning for us as it says, *"that He may grant you a spirit of wisdom and revelation* (of insight into the mysteries and secrets) *in the* (deep and intimate) *knowledge of Him, by having the eyes of your heart flooded with light, so that you can know and understand the hope to which He has called you, and how rich is His glorious inheritance in the saints* (His set-apart ones). *And* (so that you can know and understand) *what is the immeasurable and unlimited and surpassing greatness of His power in and for us who believe, as demonstrated in the working of His mighty strength."* It is in the midst of a crawl space that we discover the greatness of His power.

4
Corroded Or Corrupted In The Crawl Space

The enemy is after our word. He has been after our word since Adam and Eve. Covenant is kept by our word. God made covenant with Adam. Satan knew he could never get God to break His side of the covenant so he went after Adam's word or his side of the covenant. We all know the story. Many of us have gotten sloppy with keeping our word. We are so quick to say we are going to do something and then not follow through, but God watches over His word to perform it. If we don't intend on performing what we say we will do, we need to be still. The authority of our word becomes meaningless in the realm of the spirit and in the earth. People recognize the strength of our character by whether they can trust what we say or not. When we consistently keep our word, people know we can be trusted. It is said of trustworthy people if they tell you something "you can take it to the bank." If sometimes we keep our word and sometimes we don't, we are not taken seriously. These are the ones about whom we say, "Don't hold your breath," meaning you just can't count on them. What makes us think if we cannot be counted on in natural things, we could ever have authority in the spirit?

Failing to keep our word can be intentional or forgetful. Something more exciting might have come up, or we may be such a "yes" person that we have become so over-extended there is absolutely no way—short of superhuman strength or cloning—we could ever fulfill all of our commitments before Jesus comes. Sometimes we say "yes" simply to get the person asking to leave us alone having no intention of following through. Maybe there is recognition for saying "yes" for the moment, and seeking to be noticed is all we are after. The correlating work is not our cup of tea, so we call back after the dust has settled giving some fabricated excuse as to why we cannot fulfill our commitment with our apologies, or worse yet just not showing up. Or perhaps we are people who just don't know how to say "No" because we try to please everybody.

Sometimes forgetfulness is an issue. I have found if something is really important to me, I do not forget. I write it down sometimes in several different places and make a mental note so I won't forget. We especially remember if there is a penalty attached to forgetting the appointment. We need to be careful of committing to something that holds no value to us. If we have a propensity to forgetfulness, we need to do something to help us jog our memory.

Father, help us if we are prone to choose something else more exciting or appealing to us than keeping our word to a prior commitment. Most of the time, the alternative is only a test to see if we will keep our word in the midst of choices. Remember it is only a good test if the alternative to keeping your prior commitment is truly desirable. Commitment is only commitment in the face of multiple choices.

Then, for all of us who are prone to be "yes" people, no matter how full our plate is, we are so sure we can add one more thing. Most of the time, we don't even evaluate how full our plate really is until what is on it begins to spill over the sides. It is true that 20% of the people do 80% of the work, but the 20% need to determine their plates will not hold more than 80% capacity. Normally, however, they fill their plates 110%.

> **Commitment is only commitment in the face of multiple choices.**

Good intentions don't count in the realm of the spirit. We either kept our word or we didn't in any situation in which we gave our word. In keeping our word, we chose righteousness. Ignoring our word will cost us adhering to the standard of authority God has set in the midst of us. If we have developed a habit of not keeping our word, we need to cry out for grace to be able to keep our word and be able to stand uprightly again before God. We can no longer justify why we aren't able to keep our word if we want to move into a greater authority in the realm of the spirit. God desires to bring us to a new dimension of His glory, but He can't as long as we are resistant to His standard in our lives. God watches over His word to perform it. Jeremiah 1:12 says, *"He will hasten His word to perform it."* Being transformed into the image of God doesn't mean physically looking like God but acting like Him. If he hastens to perform His word then we ought also to keep our word.

It's Only a Test

In November of 2002 Connie and I were asked to begin a Wednesday night service in a community an hour and a half from my home. After prayer we agreed to assume the responsibility of this weekly meeting. In December of 2002, we set the date for the first Wednesday night service. It was announced to the congregation and everything was in order until . . . I received a reminder e-mail from the university I was attending to complete my master's degree. My upcoming class was scheduled for the same week I was to begin Wednesday night services.

My first thought was to postpone the start date for the Wednesday night service, but the little voice in my heart quietly said, "You gave your word. What lengths are you willing to go to keep it?" To keep my word to the church required leaving class early Wednesday afternoon. I would have to get permission from the dean of the graduate school and make up the work. It was a 6 hour drive one way to hold the service followed by the drive back in the same night to be ready for class the following morning. It was inconvenient and exhausting to keep my word. Remarkably, I was refreshed and ready for class the next day and none of my work suffered from missing that afternoon.

Many times our word bows to the "god" of convenience. If it is *convenient* I will keep my word, but if I see that I will be *inconvenienced* in any way then I don't feel obligated to my word. Now you would think that since it was so inconvenient to keep our word and we sacrificed to keep it that we would have had an incredible service that night. I can tell you what I preached but so far as experiencing a mighty move of God that night we didn't. We drove back wondering if it was worth it since we didn't see any immediate results. I am sure there are those of you reading this that can relate to this thought process and we end up believing it really didn't matter whether I kept my word or not. We have now labored there more than a year. We were told that we would never hold a crowd through the summer months, but we did. Our labor there has gained favor and a level authority that I know we would never have had if we had not kept our word. Our example and teaching of keeping our word produced the following story.

One of the ladies attending the Wednesday night services had given her word that she would be in charge of an upcoming Saturday morning event. She received a call the morning of the event concerning her mother's health. In days gone by her reaction would have been to drop her responsibility, leave everyone counting on her in a lurch, and run to her mother's aid. She remembered my teaching and example of keeping our word and put it to the test. She fulfilled her responsibilities Saturday morning and went to see her mother when she was through. Every health issue her mother was having that morning had been totally resolved by the time she got there and she was doing fine. She came the next Wednesday night filled with excitement at what God had done for her and her mother that she would not have experienced if she had not kept her word. What would the world be like if every Christian began to keep their word leaning into Almighty God to do the rest? Leaders, we cannot expect our people to keep their word if we do not lead by example. We actually teach more by example than by what we say.

Sometimes "urgent" calls simply come to test the worth of our word. Sometimes the new information seems to be the most critical, demanding immediate attention as in the case of this woman's mother. What I have found to be true over and over is if

I take care of watching over my word to perform it God will watch over my personal affairs and release His supernatural ability in my behalf. He takes care of my business so much better than I am able to do in my own ability.

Time after time "things" will come up that will tempt us to not keep our word. They will be legitimate things that carry weight and value. If they weren't it would not be a good test. The test is to see whether we will keep our word. The test goes beyond just the natural circumstances of the moment. The test is watched with great interest in the heavenlies by both the kingdom of darkness and the Kingdom of Light. We sing about "making war in the heavenlies." If we truly want to make war in the heavenlies and tear down principalities we will do it by keeping our word and gaining new levels of authority in the heavenly realm. *"Well done thou good and faithful servant; you were faithful over a few things, I will make you ruler over many things. Enter into the joy of your Lord."* (Matthew 25:21) We tend to think this only applies to the talents discussed in this story when in fact it is a principle to be applied to every area of our lives. Our faithfulness is being watched. The thing that we are least faithful with is following through with our word even down to simply returning a phone call when we say we will. *"He who is faithful in what is least is faithful also in much."* (Luke 16:10)

There is a rest that comes in learning to keep our word amidst new information. I have discovered there is no peace in continually chasing after new choices presented to try to stop me from keeping my word. The other choices always appear to be things that we alone can take care of or we absolutely can't afford to pass up this opportunity. Both are deceptions. If we think we are the only one that can take care of something then we have a higher opinion of ourselves than we ought to have. Others can take care of things and will when we aren't there to do it. They may not do things the way we would, but things will still get done. It requires a deeper trust in God Almighty to give wisdom to the "others" who are taking care of what we are not there to do, and a deeper trust that God Almighty will be our rear guard if need be

The Crawl Space

if "they" miss it. God is not just God Almighty when we are there. God is God Almighty!

There is nothing like our absence to promote growth in responsibility of those around us and our absence will eventually come. If we want what we are doing to outlive us we must impart our heart and what we know in those who will follow after us. My husband's absence due to death has caused my family to grow up into the responsibilities he left behind. My sons and I no longer have the luxury of a father and husband making decisions and overseeing our 15 acres but we have his heart and the knowledge he imparted to us. We may not do things exactly like he would if he was still here, but everything is getting done, decisions are still being made, and life certainly does go on.

> **God is God Almighty!**

Secondly, "I can't afford to pass up this opportunity" is also a deception. We think all of life rises and falls on a single moment in time. We are deceived into believing nothing this good will ever come around again. Our God is bigger than that. If we will keep our word and prove we can be trusted even when the stakes are high, He will do exceedingly abundantly above all we can ask or think. The test goes beyond what is seen in the natural. Events of life will come and go but keeping our word speaks for eternity. It proves the depth and maturity of our character.

When the enemy discovers he can break our word with new information he will continue until he keeps us in constant emotional upheaval. But when we withdraw ourselves from that loop and begin to keep our word, we step into a realm of ruling over our emotions and our schedules to a greater degree. There is a rest that comes in that and best of all we enter into the joy of the Lord.

Test it for yourself. Begin to require yourself to rise to a new level of keeping your word regardless of what it is no matter how strict you currently are. See for yourself what a difference it makes in your ministry or the atmosphere of your family. The first change you'll find is you won't be so loose with your word. When you place more value on keeping your word you won't be so cheap with where and how we throw it around. You will also find as you make a conscious decision to be more accurate with keeping your word there will come a new rush of "enticing things," "urgent things," or keeping your word will simply become "inconvenient" tempting you to call and make apologies canceling your word. Remember, your word—kept or un-kept—makes huge statements in the heavenlies for or against you, producing authority or lack of authority in your life. I repeat, "The enemy is after your word."

Corroded Pipes

Corroded galvanized pipes are a good example of what can happen over time in our relationships with other people when we don't keep our word. Our connections with other people can become clogged with offenses, hurts, and misunderstandings nearly always due to a lack of integrity in the small things. Broken promises, confidences, trust, unfulfilled expectations, anger, and dishonesty are all little rust particles that accumulate over time. Our pipe line or love line as Connie Harris, co-founder of Walk With Me Ministries describes it, can become so clogged that love can no longer flow or it only trickles to those to whom we are connected. This is how divorce eventually occurs, and those who began so head over heels in love end wondering, "Where did all the love go?" Friendships end many times for the same reason.

It is so much easier to sweep a rust particle or offense "under the rug" thinking, "I don't want to make any waves or confront this issue. I'll just go on, pretend all is okay, and just deal with my own attitude and emotions by myself." It doesn't work that way. That is the same as not dealing with it, and pretending is dishonest, corrupting our integrity. That little rust particle or offense is allowed to lodge somewhere on the inside of your heart waiting to collect another and another and

> **The enemy is after your word.**

another like particle. Instead of getting the offense out in the open, confessed and under the blood, it is cataloged in the recesses of our heart until such a time when something else occurs triggering the remembrance of all past offenses.

Sadly, we can allow the events that have caused offense in us by other people to clog our love lines without "them" even knowing. The events retained in the crevices of our minds and hearts are events of little importance and unmemorable to "them." Yet, we have allowed those events to grow bigger and bigger in our hearts by nursing them and rehearsing them until one day enough is enough. We spew out all the offenses of yesteryear as well as this last straw that broke the camel's back today. When we bring up the ones from the past and "they" don't even remember, that gives even more fuel to the fire. Thoughts like, "I'm not even important enough for them to remember that event" surface. The relationship is then ruined, not because it was unavoidable, but because offenses weren't taken care of with integrity in a timely manner.

The Bible says in Ephesians 4:26–27, *"When angry, do not sin; do not ever let your wrath* (your exasperation, your fury or indignation*) last until the sun goes down. Leave no such room or foothold for the devil* (give no opportunity to him.)*"* Another way of saying this is, "If you've been offended by something or someone, don't go to bed that night without dealing with it." If you do, you give opportunity to be hidden from one another. The enemy wants us to go to bed offended. As time passes it is easier and easier to hide the offense, allowing accumulation of offenses to build. If we could ever learn to be transparent, walking uprightly with one another instead of pretending we are so saintly that nothing anyone can do can hurt us, the enemy would have nothing in which he could get a hook in to destroy our relationships. It is the hidden things that always come to light over time with a destructive force.

The devil deceives us into believing the best thing to do in an offensive situation is just pretend all is okay. That is dishonest. No, the best thing to do is deal with the issue while it is still small (a particle of rust) before it has had a chance to grow and accumulate. If the issue seems to be small enough to be overlooked and we are able to pretend all is well, it is also small enough to be uprooted and never allowed to grow into full-blown division. The smallest issue hidden has opportunity to place a wedge of division jeopardizing the integrity of our relationships.

The smallest offense not dealt with also allows the opportunity in our hearts for the devil to cause us to walk dishonestly and deceitfully in other things. All issues of our heart are interrelated and interwoven. If a seed of division is allowed to remain unchecked in any area, it will weaken our integrity and will eventually produce corruption after its kind throughout our heart. We are admonished in Proverbs 4:23 to *"Keep and guard our heart with all vigilance and above all that we guard, for out of it flows the springs or issues of life."* The enemy would deceive us into believing it is best to guard the person that offended us or the relationship by not saying anything. Quite the opposite is true. We may have avoided the moment, but we have not guarded our heart from the accumulation of offenses. The accumulation of offenses begins to bend our hearts from being straight, clean, and pure before God and each other, and the gush of offenses that is sure to follow at some future point will be much worse than dealing with each offense as it comes.

5
Do We Avoid Or Endure The Crawl Space

The crawl space is where we only go when we have to. We usually find ourselves there as a result of ignorance, mismanagement of responsibilities, or the occurrence of events over which we have no control. Jerry and I purchased a rental house one summer from an individual who failed to inform us that during the winter months, the holes screened in around the foundation of the house needed to be closed. In our ignorance we didn't realize that needed to be done. Needless to say, when severe cold weather struck, the house wasn't ready, and the pipes burst. Jerry and I found ourselves in a brand new crawl space with a new situation we had never dealt with before. We again had a small pond; however, that time we could have had an ice rink. A potentially fun thing in the wrong place just means hard work. A real estate quote I once heard was, "Location, location, location."

Some crisis situations can occur due to a lack of discipline or management on our part. Perhaps we haven't been good stewards of our money, and credit cards and debt have inched their way to red alert. Even though it was a build up over time, one day it dawns on our understanding; we are in a crisis situation no longer able to pay our debts and we are dropped into a crawl space.

We can find ourselves in a crawl space because of poor decisions. We can choose to walk willfully disobedient to God's commands or civil law. Then we awaken to the realization that the lifestyle we have chosen has caught up with us, and we find ourselves in a dark hard place emotionally, spiritually, and physically.

Sometimes bankruptcy comes to our door by no fault of

our own. It could be because someone in debt to us defaults on what they owe causing a domino effect in our financial portfolio. Perhaps our life savings was wrapped up in a poorly managed stock option, and now our retirement years are questionable.

Maybe we chose to hang with the wrong crowd, or our children chose to hang with the wrong crowd. Events happening to our children can affect us deeper than our own personal events. We then find ourselves in a crawl space, not because of any wrong we actually committed, but because of association with disobedience.

The crisis of hearing a bad report from a doctor can drop us into a crawl space. We may have received a terminal diagnosis, or we may have sustained a debilitating accident. When Connie's husband, Lee, and my husband, Jerry, died so suddenly, 33 days apart, our pipes burst. The love that flowed so freely in our marriages poured to the ground through gaping holes, sending us into a crawl space.

> **It really doesn't matter how the crisis starts. What matters is how we end up.**

Sometimes we face events of life that are unexplainable and we simply cannot understand why they happened. We say the devil stole from us, or a door was left open for the enemy to attack us, or that simply should not have happened. This is futile thinking. It really doesn't matter how the crisis starts. What matters is how we end up. Whatever the crisis, a rupture occurs, and the integrity of the internal workings of the spirit man is challenged. The question should be how do we walk through the midst of the crisis and come out on the other side with more faith than when the crisis or crawl space experience began?

Endurance Through Suffering

We'd like to think we will be able to live our lives untouched by difficult circumstances. The truth is, difficult things in life happen to all of us, sometimes by our own making and sometimes simply because in this world we will have trouble, things hard to deal with and hard to bear. John 16:33 says, *"I have told you these things, so that in Me you may have* (perfect) *peace and confidence. In the world you have tribulation and trials and distress and frustration; but be of good cheer!* (Take courage; be confident, certain, undaunted!) *For I have overcome the world* (I have deprived it of its power to harm you and have conquered it for you.)"

We have taken this verse to mean since Jesus has already overcome the world that by our faith in Him, we will be able to breeze through life having nothing to deal with and nothing to bear. Therefore, we have developed an "avoidance" theology in regards to pain and suffering rather than a biblical "endurance" theology. However, if we are being told to "be of good cheer," the implication is that we could choose in the midst of how things appear to "not be of good cheer." When an event occurs that is hard to deal with or hard to bear, we tend to crash and burn because we do not have an "endurance through suffering" theology.

Our tendency is to ask "why?" We usually immediately begin to ask, "Why is this happening to me." Then we go down through a checklist of: "Did I leave a door open to the enemy?" "Why didn't I have enough faith?" "If I would only have . . ." "I should have . . ." "Where was God?" "Is He angry with me?" These kinds of questions only produce speculation and more questions. "Why" is not the right question! I said earlier in regards to the house, why you have to access the crawl space isn't as important as the fact that if you don't, the future comfort within the house will be affected. What?" is the question! "What am I to do in the midst of the crawl space?" The answer is "Worship!"

> **We have developed an "avoidance" theology in regards to pain and suffering rather than a biblical "endurance" theology.**

Releasing Hidden Treasures

Worship will release the hidden treasures in the darkness of the crawl space. Worship will allow God to develop maturity of character and integrity in us. Worship will change the attitude of our hearts to reflect more of who God *is* while we are in the darkness of the crawl space. Worship allows God to bring from our lives a new revelation of His glory once we are brought back out into the light by His hand. In the darkness is where we lose our self-assertiveness and our independence, and the treasures hidden in our personality begin to emerge as we lean the entirety of our personality (all of who we are) on God. God *will* bring us out of this darkness into His marvelous light forever changed by His love. We have the mistaken idea that coming out of darkness into His marvelous light is one time only and that time being when we were born again. What I have discovered is every time I have come through a difficult dark period of time in the events of my life, the light and the love

> **Whenever God is about to reveal a new dimension of His glory in our earthen vessel, many times we go through a period of suffering or a crawl space experience.**

of God is more marvelous than ever before with a greater understanding of my real identity in Christ.

You see, the glory seen in the physical is first developed behind the scenes in the spirit, even as the in-door plumbing we enjoy today must first be developed behind the scenes in the heart of the house. Whenever God is about to reveal a new dimension of His glory in our earthen vessel, many times we go through a period of suffering or a crawl space experience. The Apostle Paul was more concerned and cognitive of the basement or crawl space of the internal fundamentals of the Spirit of man than he was of the upper stories of the house or the externals of life. Continually in his writings he stresses the fundamentals and basics of integrity. He writes that his circumstances could be abased or abound;

regardless he was content. Wow! Paul is a man so assured of his righteousness and integrity before God through Christ Jesus in the inner workings of his spirit and heart that regardless of the present suffering, it was not worthy to be compared to the glory that would be revealed when he rose up out of his difficulties. (Romans 8:18) He knew that regardless of what happened to his outward man, his inward man was being renewed day by day growing and maturing into the fullness of grace and truth that was in Jesus Christ our Lord. Our paradigm of suffering will either make or break us as we journey through the events of this life.

6
Becoming The Vision In The Crawl Space

New vision sent my husband and me into the crawl space of our home in 1986. Our vision was a new addition including a bathroom facility. Water lines had to be added to support the bathroom facility. If the plumbing had not been done in the crawl space, the bathroom would have looked good with all its new fixtures and accessories, but that is all it would have been—beauty with no function. We had to go to the crawl space to add the unseen function to the visible beauty.

God gives us a vision, shows us our purpose, and suddenly it seems events of life drop us into a crawl space. What the enemy means for evil, God will use for good to shape and mold us into the image of the vision and purpose He has placed within us. It becomes our preparation process for the vision within us. Crawl space time develops the foundation, function, character, and integrity that cannot be seen, that supports the beauty of the vision that can be seen. The crawl space is the part we have never really understood and have tried to avoid at all costs, but the crawl space is what equips us to be trusted with the reality of the vision.

What we find today is many people wanting the beauty of anointing without a crawl space experience. Sometimes I think we have the mistaken idea that God will supernaturally take us from where we are to the fulfillment of the vision He has placed within us with a powerful anointing with no sweat, blood, or tears of our own. The truth is true beauty and anointing is birthed out of the midst of the crawl space. Without the crawl space outward beauty will begin to stink in a very short while. There are no shortcuts through the preparation process. In fact, God is more interested in the preparation process than in the end result. He is more interested in developing our character and integrity until we evidence the glory and character of God in all of our relationships, even in the midst of trials, tribulations, things that are hard to deal with or hard to bear, and sufferings.

Be Still and Know

When Jesus was going through hard places, *"He opened not His mouth."* We think that is the time for screaming at the devil or anything else that moves for that matter. Hard places don't go away by screaming and yelling at them. That is how spoiled children act to get their way. Hard places are overcome by a quiet, confident surrender to the Father worshipping Him regardless, methodically walking in the stillness of his peace unmovable and unshakable by suffering or things that are hard to deal with or hard to bear.

Jesus said in Matthew 10:27, *"What I say to you in the dark, tell in the light; and what you hear whispered in the ear, proclaim upon the housetops."* When we find ourselves in the darkness of circumstances it is time to be still and listen to what God has to say. When we find His presence and hear Him speak then that is what we are to declare in the light. That is the word of authority that will speak not only in our earthly circumstance but also in the realm of the spirit. Typically in dark circumstances we fail to become quiet in the presence of God. We frantically try to figure out a solution to the darkness we are in. We lose our peace, confidence, and assurance. In the midst of the darkness, *"Be Still and Know that He is God."* (Psalms 46:10) If we will worship Him in the midst of the dark until He speaks we will walk in peace, confidence, and full assurance.

One word spoken from the mouth of God can accomplish more than we could accomplish in a whole lifetime. God is interested in discovering a life fully surrendered to Him, no matter the circumstance. He is looking for those who will practice His presence listening for His whisper in their ear. He is looking for relationship not religious activity. God isn't interested in anything we can accomplish for Him.

We are more interested in getting to the fulfillment of our vision. That's when we think we will be happy. When we begin our journey toward our vision, it is all about us and what we can do for God and how we will fulfill or play the vision that God has given us, but when we come through the process of a successful crawl space, it becomes all about Him, and our relationship with Him as He plays us as the instrument of His vision. Amazingly at some point during the process the vision that was such a burning desire in us to achieve begins to fade as we discover it is not about us or what we can do. It suddenly becomes all about Him and who He is and what He has done. All we need and the only thing we desire is His presence. If others get caught in the love affair that is going on between our Father and us, so be it, but our desire is no longer for the vision but for Him. When we become dead to ourselves and alive to Him is the point where He can trust us with the vision He wants to bring through us.

In reference again to the satanic bible, the purest form of Satanism is not bowing down in worship to Satan, but living one's life in self-centeredness. The devil loves to take the vision God has given us and make it be all about us. If he can keep our focus on the success of the vision, which of course is our success, then the image of vision produced through us will be synthetic. It will be limited to what we can produce that resembles the image of what we saw the vision to be. It will be a copy, imitation, or a form of the vision but with no real power. Then we wonder why our vision doesn't seem to be producing the desired results we thought it would or should.

God isn't interested in imitation, synthetic visions. He is about the business of birthing the vision in us by causing us to understand our complete dependency on Him and His grace. It is not by our own works of righteousness. *"There is a way that seems right unto a man and appears straight before him, but at the end of it is the way of death."* Proverbs 14:12

God may have given us a vision, and we may strike out on

The Crawl Space

a way that seems the best way to us to achieve that vision. God doesn't want our best way. He wants His way. The vision cannot be produced with life and power by our righteousness or what we think is the right way. The life and power of the vision that God has given us can only be birthed, grow, finish well in our generation, and perpetuate on to the next, as we become the vision by God's grace rather than imitate it.

Making Music

Truly anointed professional musicians do not play their instruments; they are the instruments. The musician and the instrument become one. When music is produced from them, it comes from the depths of their spirits. We feel life (inspiration) coming through their music, and it moves us to the core of our being to the point we will speak for days of how the music "moved" us. When we try to imitate the vision God has given us that resembles "playing the instrument." We are trying to make it happen. But when we *become* the vision that God plays, the sound that comes from us is full of grace and truth, life and power. We become the instrument with God being the Musician producing the life and the music of the vision through us. It is not an imitation of the vision or a copy of anyone else's vision. It is an original!

We get in the midst of a tough place and decide this can't be God. We do everything we can to get out of the crawl space when God wants us to stay under his hand for the life of the vision to be produced in us. The life of the vision is the basics that the Apostle Paul knew so well. Our vision, talents, and giftings, can take us where our integrity and character cannot keep us. If we skirt the crawl spaces, we will never mature, and the life of the vision will not be produced in us. Whatever imitation or synthetic vision comes from us will not remain because it is like a cheap copy of the Mona Lisa.

When we find ourselves in a crawl space, the devil's tactic is to get us to believe God has forsaken us, or we have sinned, or we question our faith. If he is successful, we will never come out of the crawl space victoriously, and perhaps he can make us bitter against God and everyone else. God has not forsaken us. If we will just stay under the hand of God in the midst of the crawl space, we are in line for promotion to be the vision or the instrument of God. The glory to be revealed will not be worthy to be compared to the suffering because the glory will shine forth out of our lives with a purity and holiness as never before. We are set free from slavery to sin and self-centeredness instead becoming a slave to God. Our present reward now is holiness and its end is eternal life according to Romans 6:22.

A successful crawl space experience frees us from our self-centeredness. It is no longer about me or my ability. It is about God and His grace, His power, and His ability being sufficient in my life. My righteousness and leaning to my own understanding ceases to exist somewhere along the way in the darkness of the crawl space. I learn self-abandonment to God leaning all of who I am, the entirety of my personality on Him, with a personal trust, confident surrender, and a firm reliance.

Until this kind of maturity is birthed in us, we can corrupt the vision and do as much harm as good. The masses we preach to and the many that decide for Christ in our meetings are important, but the "one" that could be lost because of my acting out of self-centeredness in my personal dealings is just as important. Our lack of character and integrity in our dealings with the "one" can cause spiritual death and God is not willing that any should perish. The test of whether we *play* the instrument or whether we *are* the instrument is in our willingness to leave the masses to evidence and witness the character and integrity of God to the "one." Luke 15:4 says, *"what man of you, having a hundred sheep, if he loses one of them, does not leave the ninety-nine in the wilderness, and go after the one which is lost until he finds it? And when he has found it, he lays it on his shoulders, rejoicing. And when he comes home, he calls together his friends and neighbors, saying to them, Rejoice with me, for I have found my sheep which was lost!"*

I wonder if this is what Jesus meant in Matthew 7:22, 23 where it is written, *"Many will say to Me on that day, Lord, Lord have we not prophesied in Your name and driven out demons in Your name and done many mighty works in Your name. And then I will say to them openly* (publicly), *I never knew you; depart from Me, you who act wickedly* (disregarding My commands)." At the name of Jesus every name must bow. There is power and mighty things will happen simply in using the mighty name of Jesus, but behind the scenes of the mighty display of power of God, how do we act? Do our lives evidence the character and integrity of God or our own self-centeredness? Having said the purist form of Satanism is not bowing down in worship to Satan but living a life of self-centeredness, it follows that the purist form of Christianity is not ONLY bowing in worship to God but presenting our bodies a living sacrifice unto Him in self-abandonment living a sacrificial life, displaying Christ-likeness in thought, word, and deed to many or to one, no matter where we are or what we are doing. Only by leaning into the grace of our Lord Jesus Christ and His sacrifice can we do this.

We have never understood what Paul meant in Romans 8:17 when he said, *"Only we must share His suffering if we are to share His glory."* Suffering doesn't necessarily have to be taking stripes on your back. Actually we may have difficulty enduring actual physical abuse for the "cause of Christ" if we can't endure suffering a little inconvenience with a good attitude.

According to Romans 5:3, 4 Paul says, *"Let us be full of joy now! Let us exult and triumph in our troubles and rejoice in our sufferings, knowing that pressure and affliction and hardship produce patient and unswerving endurance. And endurance* (fortitude) *develops maturity of character* (approved faith and tried

> **Hardships aren't to punish us but to produce patience, endurance, mature character, and confident hope of eternal salvation.**

integrity). *And character of this sort produces the habit of joyful and confident hope of eternal salvation. Such hope never disappoints or deludes or shames us, for God's love has been poured out in our hearts through the Holy Spirit Who has been given to us."* Hardships aren't to punish us but to produce patience, endurance, mature character, and confident hope of eternal salvation.

Securing The Joints

In the crawl space of a house, the integrity of each joint has to be made secure. Each pipe has to be methodically connected in proper order. Distances and angles have to be measured out. The proper grade for removing sewer waste has to be maintained so it doesn't move too fast or slow. All the pipes have to be well supported to insure the integrity of the system. If shortcuts are taken, we're sure to find ourselves back in the crawl space doing it again at some point in the future. The same holds true in the Spirit.

> **When God wants to do a new thing in us or change the direction of our ministry, He prepares us in the crawl space.**

In the crawl spaces of life, if we will look close enough, we'll discover that every event the enemy meant for our harm God will orchestrate for our good. We find out just how frail and weak we are and discover our dependency on the grace of God. When God wants to do a new thing in us or change the direction of our ministry, He prepares us in the crawl space. Each new stage requires new training and deeper surrender. Without proper preparation, the new vision will collapse but crawl spaces certainly aren't easy.

7
Crawl Spaces Prove What We Are Made Of

The crawl space in the old part of our house constructed in the 1800's could not even be called a crawl space. The original builders were either midgets or conserved their energy when it came to moving dirt. In some places the crawl was a belly scoot resembling what I have seen of army training where they move forward by elbows and toes under low barbed wire. Many places my husband was too large to fit in the old construction. We wanted an additional phone line in the far end of the old part of our house. Actually I wanted the new line and Jerry wasn't too excited about all the work it would take to get the job done. Can any other ladies out there relate to that? Of course, the same holds true when our husbands have an idea and we don't share their enthusiasm. This, of course, was in my non-pregnant days, but vision once again sent me under the house.

To me a job worth doing is worth doing well, and draping a phone cord along the outside of the interior walls to get to the room where the phone was to go just wouldn't do. To accomplish this task, once I got into the crawl space, I had a long belly crawl ahead of me under low hanging heating and air conditioning ducts. I literally had to drag myself with my elbows or inch my way pushing forward with the toes of my shoes with my head turned sideways in the dirt to make it through the compressed passage way—not a good place to be if you are claustrophobic. Actually, it was just not a good place to be and terribly uncomfortable.

My pants got caught on a piece of metal hanging down from the heating and cooling ductwork. It was difficult to say the

The Crawl Space

least to maneuver enough to release my pants from its grip, but not before it had left its mark on me and my pants. Once I made it under the duct work, I found that the room where I was headed was also an earlier addition, and I was up against an old concrete foundation. At first my heart sank. Suddenly I saw phone cord draped along the outside of interior walls. There was no way equipment to break through the old foundation would ever fit in this crawl space without a lot of digging. I continued to scoot along the foundation and discovered someone else had cut a hole through the foundation in a previous day barely large enough from side to side to slip through, so a new squeeze was on. Finally arriving at the place we wanted the new phone line, I poked the phone wire up through the hole we had pre-drilled from above and made my way back out through the same difficult passageways. It was a slow, difficult process—very constrictive.

Maybe God has given us a vision of communicating the gospel to a new people group no one has ever ministered to before or maybe God has given us a new message to deliver, but the ground work to reach the "far side of the house" or that new people group has to be laid. We may get hung up on a nail as we pass through difficult places, and it may leave its mark on us. Hebrews admonishes us to strip down and lay aside every weight that so easily besets us. In tight places, looseness in our character will be revealed and hinder our progress in the vision set before us. God calls us to lay aside the weights or "loose living" that so easily trips us up that His glory might be revealed. (Hebrews 12:1)

Crawl spaces really prove what we are made of and if the vision will really become a reality. Some abort the vision in the crawl space because the humility of having our face in the dirt and the narrowness of the passageways that demand we strip off some things that are important to us is too hard. The degree of glory to be visibly revealed in the house is relative to the degree of darkness and difficulty beneath the house in the crawl space.

Sometimes you have to go it alone
It is in the crawl spaces of life we learn to lean the entirety

of who we are on God. In those tight places, no one else can come through with us. They may go before us as someone else had done in making a hole in the foundation in a previous age or generation so I could pass through, or they may come behind us in future generations with another new vision that God has given them to build upon what has already been laid. Every generation builds upon the last with the new vision God is giving in the current day, but to make the new vision a reality we each must come through a crawl space alone with our Father God.

Having been in a crawl space, we become more sensitive and compassionate in praying for others who are in a crawl space. In days gone by, we have tended to be quick to judge when others were in a crawl space because of lack of understanding of what it was to accomplish in their lives. Our judging has caused the abortion of many God-given visions. We haven't understood that if the glory of the Lord is to be revealed in the earth we must learn steadfast, patient endurance in the midst of a crawl space experience. We who are not in the crawl space need what will be revealed through the lives of those who come successfully through the crawl space under the hand of God. Whenever God does something in the life of a person, it is for the benefit of many.

Instead of judging people as to why they are in a crawl space and declaring if they just had enough faith (like me) they wouldn't be there, we need to encourage them in the midst of the crawl space and pray that they will diligently develop into what God is doing in them until the end. There is always one more thing about a person we do not know that makes our judgment false. We don't know what glory will be revealed in a person's life once they successfully complete the crawl space experience, but the glory revealed upon their exit will serve to nourish and bless others; even those critical of their descent into the crawl space.

Don't Give Up

Sometimes the crawl space we are dropped into spiritually feels like the circumstances I found myself in under the old part of our house. It can feel like we are inching along on our belly with our cheek in the dust pressed to the ground. It can feel like we are getting nowhere fast. It can seem so hard; particularly when we have to have the tools we need to work with when we get to where we are going, so we are not only moving ourselves through the constricted pass but sometimes dragging something necessary with us. Our backs may be rubbing against the constriction above us. It may feel so tight we feel we cannot get through. We begin to think, "I'll just settle for wrapping the house up in phone cord."

If our vision is only for comfort and beauty without an understanding of the crawl space experiences, we won't get through. We will give up and quit. It is the crawl space experience that develops the character and the integrity to support the beauty of the vision that soon will become visible for all to see.

Birthing New Life

Matthew 7:13, 14 says, *"Enter through the narrow gate; for wide is the gate and spacious and broad is the way that leads away to destruction, and many are those who are entering through it. The gate is narrow* (contracted by pressure) *and the way is straitened and compressed that leads away to life, and few are those who find it."* The vision is placed within us, but then we are led away to the narrow gate. If we go through the narrow gate and stay under the hand of God, the vision that was placed in us will birth into life. It must first become life to us before it can become life-giving to others. God immediately goes about birthing the very life of the vision in us. If left to ourselves, we will produce the form or image of the vision, and there will be no life or power in it. Those that eat of our fruit will also be lifeless and powerless. But if we stay under the hand of God through the crawl space, the life of the vision will be produced in us. Then those who eat of the fruit of the vision will also receive the life and the power of God.

Keep the Vision Alive

Sometimes we *"have a form of godliness but denying the*

power thereof." (II Timothy 3:5) Man has a lot of ability. We can truly create a replica of the image of the vision that God has given us by our own ability. It looks like the vision we saw. It has a form of godliness because it is created by our image of what we think righteousness to be in our vision. Actually, we produce a good synthetic or copy of the original vision. Synthetic visions produce synthetic children. Synthetic can make us feel good and give us an emotional high for the moment, but God's grace (power and ability to change us) will only show up in the reality of the vision. The reality of the vision is only produced when it ceases to be all about us.

We have fought the crawl space with everything available in our faith artillery. Dark, ugly places certainly could not be God's will for our lives. We have tried to use our faith against the crawl space rebuking the enemy of darkness from our lives when actually it could be God orchestrating our circumstances to facilitate a new depth of understanding of character and integrity. He does this to support a new, beautiful anointing, which He wants to make operative in our lives to reveal more of His glory. When God introduces a new glory it requires a new level of integrity to support the glory.

Somehow experiencing crawl space time has a way of making us more sensitive to others who tell us of the crawl space experience they are currently facing. Unless you have experienced the crawl space, you don't have a real perspective of what it is like and genuine compassion is lacking. Yes, we can be dropped into a crawl space for any number of reasons. We may have opened the door to the enemy or made wrong choices. None of us are exempt from that. As soon as we think we are exempt from being untouched by life and innocent of all evil doing, look out. It is only by the grace of God that any of us stand.

This Doesn't Look Like the Promise Land

It may be just the facts of life itself. Life happens! A very real fact of life is as long as there is heaven and earth; there will be pain, suffering, sickness, and even death. It may not even be

The Crawl Space

our own personal pain or suffering. It may be pain, difficult circumstances, sickness, or death of someone we are closely related to that drops us into the crawl space. The unexpected death of our husbands certainly dropped Connie and I into a crawl space. No matter how long someone we love lives, it is never long enough if we are the person left behind. There is grief and loss to bear.

For many years we have believed if we had enough faith, we would never find ourselves in the midst of real life. Our shoes would never wear out (referring to the children of Israel in the wilderness) and we would have comfort all the days of our lives. When this doesn't happen, we wonder what is wrong with us and where did we go wrong. Actually, if we have enough faith, we will go through the hardships and struggles of real life in confidence and serene peace based on the grace (the ability and power) of our Father. Children panic and run in fear. A mature saint of God is so coherent of the integrity and character of God within him that it matters very little what is going on in his external happenings. He is more coherent of his internal being than he is of the outward struggles. The mature saint has spent enough time in crawl spaces to know that the integrity of his temple is intact. His outward flesh no longer rules him, but he is ruled by his spirit man full of grace and truth.

It has occurred to me what a gracious and merciful God we serve in reading again for the first time the wilderness experience of the children of Israel. If their shoes were to have worn out in their 40-year trek in the wilderness it would surely have compounded their problems to have sore feet. I'm not sure it was their faith that kept their shoes intact as much as it was God's mercy. They had comfort. Every day they had fresh manna to eat simply by collecting it. There is nothing said of any work being done or progress being made. They simply wandered around with all their needs met waiting to live out their natural life, so the next generation could go in and possess the promise land.

Every time the Israelites were put in a position where they found themselves in a crawl space or discomfited in the wilderness, they turned to murmuring and complaining about their circumstances. They had no integrity, character, or personal reliance on God. They had no patience or endurance and weren't about to develop any. As soon as they experienced a little hunger, they cried out against Moses saying, *"Would to God we had died by the hand of the Lord in the land of Egypt. When we sat by the fleshpots and ate bread to the full; for you have brought us out into this wilderness to kill this whole assembly with hunger."* (Exodus 16:3) Oh, for goodness sake! Death is death no matter if you are full or hungry, and none of it is pleasant. But somehow in their minds, it would be much more pleasant to die full than hungry.

The events in our lives that unsettle our comfort surrendered under the hand of God can develop character. He wants to equip us for the next level of glory. He wants to introduce through our life a new revelation of His glory in the earth. We have made having our needs met the object of our faith and a sign of arrival to "great faith." If that is the case the Israelites arrived in the wilderness. Sadly, they had not arrived. God had stopped dealing with them to develop His character in them and trust in Him. If Moses had not interceded in their behalf saying, "If You are going to kill them, You'll have to kill me also," God would have wiped them out. Instead they simply lived out the rest of their lives with all the food they wanted to eat for the gathering, all their needs met, nothing wore out, and they had no enemies to face until they all died off with the exception of two scrappers—Joshua and Caleb. God by His mercy allowed another generation to come on the scene.

This new generation had a vision that didn't stop with their needs being met and nothing wearing out. They had their eyes on possessing a land flowing with milk and honey. They were focused on pulling down all the kingdoms of "ites" standing in the way of possessing a land flowing with milk and honey re-establishing the righteousness of God in the earth. They were interested in the promise land knowing the name of their God and His glory being revealed through their lives. They weren't afraid of the crawl spaces of difficulty, and their integrity and character distinctly stood out from among the rest. Even at the ripe old age of 85, Caleb said give me my mountain. He was as strong as the day he was 40 and would not be denied what his peers refused to possess because the crawl spaces were "too hard."

    Maybe we have endured our 40 years of wilderness being content with just prosperity and comfort, which is a very real and necessary aspect of faith but not an end in itself. It should be a gateway to the next step of faith on the horizon—possessing the land. We never come to the end of anything that is of God. Maybe there is a new generation on the horizon that will go a step further and possess the land. The current occupants of the promise land in the days of Moses had possessed the land. They were living quite nicely in the land. They had planted, harvested, and subdued the land in which they lived. So why should the occupancy change if there is not going to be a difference in how the land is possessed? The children of Israel had all their needs supernaturally met in the wilderness. God blessed them even though they had been rebellious towards Him. They were nomadic but seemed to enjoy it. The "ites" were comfortable in their kingdoms so why mix it up? Why change occupancy in the Promise Land if it was only going to continue under the rule of humanity. God is looking for a people who aren't content with just being occupants of a land but who will truly be surrendered to His divine rule and authority and will redeem the land to His divine rule and authority.

    I wonder if we even know what possessing the land will look like. I wonder if we know the kind of integrity and character it will take to reveal the glory of God in the earth. I wonder if we are on the brink of a generation who will be willing and obedient to find out just what it does take to reveal the glory of God in the earth and re-establish His divine rule and authority in our individual lives. I wonder if this is the generation that will finally say it is not about me or what I want but it is about You and the establishment of Your Kingdom in the earth. You are the Master Builder. You hold the Master Blue Print of what Your purpose and intention is for the entire scheme of things from the beginning of time to the end of time. I submit myself to Your plan and purpose

You have for me. Do with me as You will that Your glory be revealed in the earth through me. I wonder if this could be the generation that will cease to worship Satan with self-centeredness and will truly establish our hearts in Christ-likeness—truly eating the good of the land flowing with milk and honey. Imagine for just a moment. What will that look like?

8
Surrender In The Crawl Space

If you will remember my story in the first chapter, I was very pregnant, very heavy, and could not get out of the crawl space on my own. I tried over and over to exit the space to no avail. Frustration was setting in. How many times we have been in a crawl space of life and exhausted ourselves trying to get out by our own efforts. The crawl space in all of our lives is designed for one ultimate reason—to place our dependency solely upon God completely surrendering ourselves to Him.

Faith is our personal surrender to the Father in the midst of all of our circumstances whether they are good or bad. We have had the mistaken notion that if our circumstances are good, then that proves we have great faith, and if our circumstances are bad, then we didn't pray enough, or have enough faith, or we opened the door to the enemy somewhere. Our faith cannot be based on our circumstances whether they are good or bad. Our faith has to be based on the love of God regardless of our circumstances. In the midst of the crawl space, we must learn to surrender to Him.

Our attitude toward crawl space experiences has been to try to avoid them at all costs. That produces a people with a form of outward beauty, but under closer scrutiny their character is weak. Gifts or talents can take us where our character cannot keep us. Sometimes our glory rests upon our gifts, talents, and abilities and we catapult into service before the integrity behind the scenes is assured. We have elevated talents and abilities many times mistaking natural polish for spiritual anointing because of our lack of maturity in discernment.

Total Surrender–I worship

When our husbands died 33 days apart, it seemed as though everything Connie and I were died with them as well as all the dreams we had of what we planned to do in the future as we grew old together. Suddenly my talents and abilities didn't matter anymore. Out of my spirit came the faltering cry, "I'm at Your mercy! If You don't bring me up, Father, I am done." The story of my crawl space experience at nine months pregnant came to my mind. The only way I could come out of the crawl space in 1986 was by surrendering totally to my husband and allowing him to pull me through. We began to understand that the only thing that would bring us up out of this crawl space experience was total surrender to the Father.

Out of our spirits came a fragile gasp of the words, "I worship." Those words led to, "I surrender." With much frailty we lifted our hands and our spirits to our Father. Only as God's grace would give us strength could we even do that. Our life and our strength was totally dependent upon His grace and mercy. Even as Jerry pulled me so slowly through the access hole so many years before, it has also been a slow process out of the crawl space our husbands' deaths dropped us into. God's grace has enabled us to discover many treasures along the way.

All that has ever been of any value to the Father is the surrender of our will to Him. Sometimes we can think it is such a blessing for us to be able to use our talents and abilities for God. I had consecrated my abilities to Him and was very active in all manner of church work. What I discovered is talent and ability is no problem for God, and nothing we can do can ever "WOW!" Him. He can put what He wants in anyone or anything He wants. What sets us apart and makes us valuable to Him is our surrendered will. One would think if we have consecrated everything we can do to be used for the Lord that our will would be surrendered to Him; however, our will goes much deeper than our talents and abilities. Our will goes all the way to our attitude and motive as to why we are doing something. Most of what we do comes out of an undercurrent of "What's in it for me?"

Here is a scenario of what frequently happens when God births a vision or speaks a word in us. We see the vision or hear the word and it is glorious. We immediately set out to produce the image of the vision we saw for the world to see. God begins to use circumstances to mold us into the vision. We can choose to stay in His processing, surrendering ourselves to Him, or continue in the busyness of good things. Obedience to the voice of the Lord nearly always requires change and change many times will send us into a crawl space as the metamorphosis of the new vision is produced. Our obedience will cost those around us. When we cease to do what others have been accustomed to us doing, it triggers a domino effect. Since none of us like change, we do everything we can to avoid it.

If we would only see that we must have the crawl space experience to produce the new level of glory God wants to reveal in our lives. Paul says the sufferings (of the crawl space) *"are not worthy to be compared to the glory that will be revealed."* Romans 8:18 Crawl spaces produce character and character reveals glory.

We're Not Meant to Live in the Crawl Space

Many years ago it was told there was a family who lived in a house with a crawl space accessible through a cellar area. Occasionally when they would go to the cellar they would notice the door closing off the crawl space would be open. They would close the door only to find it to be open again and again. Food came up missing as well. After some time had passed they

> **Crawl spaces produce character and character reveals glory.**

discovered the man who had been living in the crawl space of their home helping him self to the main part of the house when they were asleep or gone and caught him. When they entered the crawl space they found his living arrangements including a mat that he slept on. What a horrible feeling it was for them to discover their privacy had been violated and what a horrible place for a human being to live.

Not everyone comes through the crawl space successfully. Some stay perpetually all the days of their lives in the crawl space unwilling to surrender everything to the Father, choosing to live their own way. Surrender to the Father is all that will bring us through. Leaning the whole of our personality upon Him and allowing Him to be the Sovereign Lord of our lives is what brings us through the crawl space. The children of Israel refused to surrender their will to God in the wilderness, and that generation died in the wilderness (crawl space). Again I ask, "Why dispossess the occupants of the promise land if the character of the people that are intended to possess it is no different from the present occupants." They murmured and complained and refused to surrender their will to God.

We have rebuked the crawl space in the name of Jesus. We have called it a demonic attack. We have labeled it "Oh ye of little faith." We have tried to get some juicy sin material on another when all the time it was a time of preparing for promotion to a new level of the glory of God in their lives. The crawl space is to cause us to become more progressively and intimately acquainted with our Father God. Remember, after Jerry pulled me through the access hole, I had a new profound respect for his strength and his ability. We have to go through some things with God and others in order for us to gain an experiential respect and trust for who they are. Talk is cheap, but when we actually put our money where our mouth is during a time of testing, all parties involved know what everyone else is made of.

Jerry loved me, and he carefully lifted me out of that hole and sat me on the floor. He didn't love me any less for being stuck in the crawl space, needing his strength to get out. He didn't love me any less for being covered from head to toe with the ugliness of the crawl space. Our heavenly Father doesn't love us any less while we are in the midst of a crawl space experience, nor does He love us any less because of the circumstances that put us there. God really isn't concerned with why we are in the crawl space.

People want to know why so we can add that into our avoidance theology. It's arrogant to believe we can become perfected without processing. God is concerned with the end result. He is after our surrender completely dependent upon Him, so He can carefully lift us out of the hole into which events of life have put us.

We can discover in the midst of the crawl space that nothing can separate us from the love of God, and we discover more intimately who God is in the midst of the crawl space. Our surrender to Him becomes more complete, and we gain dependency upon His grace. Confidence comes in our hearts because we have been taken through the crawl space; however, it is not an independent confidence, but a dependent confidence on the Father as we discover it was not by our strength but by the strength of God. He will never leave us or forsake us. *"He will never fail us or give us up or leave us without support. He will not leave us helpless or relax His hold on us. So we take comfort and are encouraged and confidently and boldly say, 'The Lord is my helper. I will not be seized with alarm* (I will not fear or dread or be terrified). *What can man do to me?'"* (Hebrews 13:5–6) When we begin to understand experientially the love of God, no matter what the circumstance, we begin to know the ability of our Father more than the ability of man. Like David, we will come to the understanding that God *is* Greater than any giant or crawl space I will ever face.

9
The Crawl Space Is Boot Camp

Life will drop us into crawl spaces. The saint understands nothing happens to us by accident, and God will orchestrate all our circumstances according to His sovereign will and purpose for our lives if we will worship. What we have failed to understand is that He is more interested in our character and integrity than He is in our comfort. We can choose to stay in the wilderness or allow God to produce His character and integrity in us, so we become redeemers in the land. We spend all kinds of time and money on education to develop skill, and we spend all kinds of time and money to make sure we look good. But as soon as circumstances come our way that God can use to orchestrate the develop our character, we cut and run.

We can't lay hands on people in a prayer line and impart character and integrity into them. We can lay hands on people and ask for the Holy Spirit to infill them, but the fruit of the evidence of the infilling of the Holy Spirit has to be walked out in real life. Evidence of character is revealed only in application, and application is by the choices we make.

Isaiah 40:31 says, *"They that wait upon the Lord shall renew their strength. They shall mount up with wings as eagles. They shall run and not be weary. They shall walk and not faint."* We all love the times of the spectacular mounting up with wings as eagles. It is easy to evidence the character of God in our lives when we come under His supernatural anointing. The times we are allowed to run unhindered with no one or nothing getting in our way are terrific too, however, it takes a special strength that only God can give to walk and not faint in the midst of a crawl space. When day in and day out it is dark, dirty, and full of cobwebs and nothing is going right, it is a little harder to evidence the character of God, but that is where the real test of character is.

When we have been running along unhindered, and we feel like we could continue forever with energy to spare, and suddenly a roadblock appears in our path, what does our character reveal and what choices do we make? A roadblock is any event of life that hinders what we envision the progress and the direction of our life to be. Our run on our journey of life may slow to a walk. Depending on the severity of the roadblock, it could become a crawl or stop completely for a time. The process of life will produce roadblocks now and then.

The term "walk" refers to character. Jesus said, "Walk before me." Live a life of integrity before me. "Walk With Me Ministries" was birthed out of the crawl space of the "shadow of death." Connie and I were taken to the depths of despair through events beyond our control. In the midst of the darkness, our Father did not leave us alone. He raised us up as we surrendered ourselves to Him. God is asking us to walk with Him in the midst of whatever the circumstance may be. He is asking us to surrender all we are to His Lordship. The hardest thing we will ever do is surrender all of who we are completely and totally to Him. That goes against everything that is in us that says we have to be somewhat in control. God is asking that we walk before Him in His character and integrity and in the image of who He is. The only way that it is possible is by surrendering ourselves to Him for Him to produce Himself in us. When our run slows to a walk or a crawl, it is development time. Integrity, character, and the fruit of the Spirit are being developed into a deeper grace in our lives. When we begin running and mounting up with eagles again, the new glory will outshine the former days before the crawl space experience.

Remember I was nine months pregnant when my husband pulled me out of the crawl space. Only 33 hours later, the "dead weight" of my body in the crawl space, helpless to get out myself, delivered new life. As we surrender to the Father, giving all of who we are to Him, becoming dead to ourselves, dependent upon Him, knowing we are unable to help ourselves, He will produce new life through us. The death that happens to us in the crawl space transforms our walk before Him into resurrection life when surrendered to the Father. All He needs to begin to draw us up out of the hole is our personal surrender to Him. That is faith, and faith (our personal surrender) is what pleases God.

God is developing a body of believers who have come successfully through the crawl space by the grace and mercy of God. We are a people who will not think it strange when life drops us into a crawl space, but we will surrender to the Father in the midst of the crawl space. There we allow Him to develop the new level of integrity and character that is needed in us to support the new level of glory. This glory is yet to be revealed redeeming the land. We are an army that will not be as the Israelites who were more concerned with the comfort they had left in Egypt than walking before the Father in surrender to His word regardless of the circumstances. We are the next generation army who won't mind if our comfort is unsettled if the character to possess the land births forth. We are the generation who will say, "It isn't about us and our comfort. It is about Him and His glory being revealed in the earth." We really have no idea what the next level of glory will look like. All we know is we want it. All we know is it is not about us anymore, but it is all about Him.

It will take a greater level of integrity to come into the next generation anointing.

It will take a greater level of integrity to come into the next generation anointing. Don't think it strange if we find ourselves in a crawl space. God has a vision of what He wants us to be when our crawl space experience is through. He knows the seed of destiny He has placed within us. He is preparing His army to bear the next level of glory in the earth and possess the land. So don't fight the crawl space. Embrace it! Let it take you deep into the intimate knowledge of who God is. Turn the tables on the enemy.

Boot Camp

In the midst of this crawl space compassion for others will saturate our lives. Maybe we should say the crawl space is army boot camp. Army personnel have a mutual respect for each other having gone through the same grueling training to produce the caliber of people required by the armed forces. They don't point their fingers at others in process to try to figure out why they are in training. They know they are in training to become qualified people. We just haven't understood in the Christian army that the crawl spaces are the boot camp of our lives to produce a higher quality of integrity, character, discipline, and maturity. There is coming an army that is so surrendered to the will of the Father that they are leaning all of who they are on Him. We are this army of believers filled with the love of God. Our faith or our personal surrender to the Father God will change us from simply occupying the land to becoming redeemers of the land in our sphere of influence.

There is a groan beginning to sound among God's creation. It is a cry for the glory of the Lord to be revealed over the whole earth as the waters cover the sea. We cry out for this glory not knowing what it will be like or how it will manifest. Songs today are resounding the cry with words of "Show us your glory Lord. Let your goodness pass before us, right before our eyes." Some are looking for a supernatural manifestation of the glory of God—an extremely white bright glorious light coming from the throne of God illuminating all the earth. Others may see the glory of God causing our faces to shine as He caused the face of Moses to shine after he had been on the mountaintop with God. If we have given the glory of God much thought at all, we will each have preconceived ideas as to what it will be, but none of us really know what seeing the glory of God will really be like. I just have some food for thought.

A man's character is his glory or his shame. He is known for his integrity or the lack of it. Could it be that the revelation of the glory of God will begin to be seen in the body of Christ as His character is revealed in their everyday mundane dealings with "creation?" We all love the mountaintop experiences ranging from our private time with God to a wonderfully inspired and anointed corporate meeting with other members of the body of Christ. That is where we see and experience the glory of God, but then we must be able to walk it out in the valley or where the rubber meets the road in our lives.

Mountaintop to Mountaintop

We find the story of the Mount of Transfiguration in Matthew 17 parallels with our experiences from time to time. How amazing it is that we can have a wonderful time of prayer and intimacy with the Father only to have a situation arise that changes our glorious mount of transfiguration experience with the Lord to "dungeons and dragons" in a heartbeat. We see the glory of God and touch the glory of God with our emotions, but we have not learned to descend from those wonderful times of experiencing the glory of God and live it in the ordinary mundane facts of life.

We have gone to wonderful meetings and conferences for both men and women. The atmosphere is supercharged with the corporate anointing that is in the house. Our emotions are touched even as Peter's was on the mount of transfiguration and we want to build three tabernacles and just live right there where there are no challenges never going home. When Jesus, Peter, James, and John came down from the mountain they were greeted by a crowd of people who had brought an epileptic boy to be healed. We know when we go home chances are we will lose the emotion of the moment by being thrust again into our "crowd" of people who may be faithless, stubborn, and sometimes even thoroughly perverse even as Jesus described the crowd He descended to. How do we live for the glory of God that we have seen on the mountain top in the midst of the valley?

We tend to want to live life as a movie. A movie is life with all the dull parts cut out. Our lives are made up of many more mundane, dull, commonplace moments than mountain top experiences; yet, we spend our lives seeking mountaintop experiences to the neglect of embracing the walk with God in the valley among the "crowd" revealing the glory we have seen on the mountain. I personally have come home from meetings expecting the "crowd" I descended among to recognize that I had had a mountaintop experience, and they would know by my very face that the glory of God was upon me. Nobody did! They were exactly as I had left them and treated me exactly as they had before I went to the meeting. Nothing changed except my "glow faded and I lived for the next meeting.

Valley to Valley

Instead of living to see the glory of God from meeting to meeting we need a paradigm shift. What would happen if we would begin to "be" the glory of God from valley to valley amongst our "crowd" of people? Jesus continued to be the glory of God through his walk in the valley. His living, His actions, and His words revealed the very character of God. If our being in the presence of God in a mountain top experience doesn't change us, then we are still into "modified behavior." The only way we will begin to reflect His image and His character is by being dependent upon God's grace, His power and His ability, to get us where we need to be. That demands a continual surrendering of our will to His will, even in the midst of the pressure of the "crowd."

When the disciples came to Jesus and asked Him why they could not cure the boy, His reply was, *"Because of the littleness of your faith* (that is, your lack of firmly relying trust)." Let's look at some historical accounts of real people who stood the pressure of the crowd in the valley of real life events and became redeemers in their sphere of influence as they surrendered themselves in firmly relying trust upon God.

10
Gideon's Crawl Space

The story of Gideon is found in Judges Chapters 6–8. Gideon was threshing wheat in the winepress to hide from the Midianites who were impoverishing the people of Israel. An Angel of the Lord came to him and said, *"The Lord is with you, you mighty man of fearless courage."* (6:12) The angel goes on to say that Gideon is to deliver Israel from the hand of the Midianites.

The Lord said, *"Go in this your might, and you shall save Israel from the hand of Midian. Have I not sent you?"* (6:14)

Gideon replies, *"Oh Lord, how can I deliver Israel? Behold, my clan is the poorest in Manasseh, and I am the least in my father's house."* (6:15)

The Lord said to him, *"Surely I will be with you, and you shall smite the Midianites as one man."* (6:16)

The angel of the Lord continued to give Gideon instruction. He told him to take the 2nd bull from his father, Joash's, herd that was 7 years old and pull down the idol of Baal that his father had with the goddess that was beside it. Then he was supposed to build an altar to the Lord on top of this stronghold with stones laid in proper order and offer the bull with the wood of the idols as a burnt offering. The story of Gideon is so symbolic of the coming New Covenant God would make through his Son Jesus Christ. The 2nd bull represents the 2nd man, Adam, who was Jesus Christ, the Son of the Living God. The number 7 represents perfection, completion, and bringing to an end. Wood represents the sin of humanity. Jesus Christ was the perfect sacrifice that completed the need for any future sacrifices, consuming the sin of humanity, fulfilling or completing the Old Covenant and establishing the New.

Gideon was afraid to do this in daylight, so he took 10 of his servants and accomplished the task at night. The next day the men of the city were furious when they discovered their idols had been destroyed. When they found out who did it, they wanted Gideon brought out and killed. Joash instead renamed his son. Gideon was called Jerubbaal, meaning, "Let Baal contend against him, because he had pulled down his altar." Great! Having followed the Lord's direction Gideon's dad changed his name to allow Baal to curse him.

But the Spirit of the Lord clothed Gideon with Himself and took possession of him, and he blew a trumpet, and the clan of Abiezer was gathered to him as well as Manasseh, Asher, Zebulun, and Naphtali. 32,000 men gathered to the "least of the tribe of Manasseh." The Lord said to Gideon, *"The people who are with you are too many for Me to give the Midianites into their hands, lest Israel boast about themselves against Me, saying My own hand has delivered me."* This sounds so much like Ephesians 2:8–9 where Paul writes, *"For it is by grace you have been saved, through faith-and this not from yourselves, it is the gift of God-not by works, so that no one can boast."* Through the story of Gideon, God is declaring His grace.

Everyone who was afraid was told to go home. 22,000 people left. 10,000 were still too many. So the Lord told Gideon to take the people down to the water and He would test them there. Depending on how they drank from the water determined who would be chosen for Gideon's army. The army went from 32,000 to 300. Then the Lord told Gideon to surround the Midianites. What an impossible situation. They were outnumbered at 32,000 according to theologians 4 to 1, and now God says surround them with 300?!

The Lord told Gideon if he was afraid to go down to the Midianites, take a servant and sneak into the camp and hear what the Midianites have to say. "Afraid? Which tent?" Gideon and his servant went down to the camp of Midian where it was described that the men were like locusts for multitude, and their camels were without number, as the sand of the seashore for multitude. But when Gideon got to the camp, he overheard one of the men telling a dream he had had to a comrade. *"I dreamed a dream, and behold, a cake of barley bread tumbled into the camp of Midian and came to the tent and struck it so that it fell, and turned it upside down so that the tent lay flat" His comrade replied, "That is nothing else but the sword of Gideon son of Joash, a man of Israel, Into his hand God has given Midian and all the host." Gideon was strengthened when heard this conversation and worshiped the Lord.* (Judges 7:13–15)

The Bread of Life

Oh the significance of the loaf of bread. Jesus Christ is that "Loaf of Bread" the Bread of Life that has rolled into the camp of our "enemies." *"We don't wrestle against flesh and blood but against principalities and powers and the rulers of the darkness of this world."* (Ephesians 6:10–12) Like Gideon when we hear what the enemy is saying about the Bread of Life coming on the scene in our lives, we will worship. The powers of darkness tremble when we dare to believe in and surrender ourselves completely to the Bread of Life. They know their camp will be flattened and turned upside down having no more power against us.

The sacrament of communion is so important. Every time we eat the bread and drink the cup, we are representing and proclaiming the fact of the Lord's death. We need to recognize with great appreciation the deliverance that the body and the blood represent and not be careless and

> **The powers of darkness tremble when we dare to believe in and surrender ourselves completely to the Bread of Life.**

unbelieving in our participation of the sacrament. If we will understand and believe that the death, burial, and resurrection of our Lord Jesus Christ delivered us from sin's dominion (even as Gideon believed when he heard the loaf of bread rolled into the camp of his enemies and it would deliver Israel from Midian's dominion) we will find ourselves living in the supernatural realm of God's grace. No longer will we be weak in our flesh, sickly, and controlled by our flesh, but we will find ourselves controlled by the Spirit. Remember Gideon was clothed with the Spirit of God and possessed by the Spirit of God because he believed the word of the Lord and believed the loaf of bread would roll into the camp of Midian delivering them into his hand.

We are required to believe on the Lord Jesus Christ to be saved or delivered from all unrighteousness. There is no other way. When we partake of the body and the blood in communion, we need to examine ourselves and discover the enemies of righteousness in our souls and believe in the body and the blood of our Lord Jesus Christ which is represented by the bread and wine we are holding in our hands to deliver us from all unrighteousness. It is not by our works that we are delivered but by His grace. Gideon followed instruction given to him by the Lord as to what his part was in the deliverance, but the battle was the Lord's.

The Sacrament of Communion

If you attend a church that doesn't participate in the sacrament of communion with regularity, take it upon yourself to receive communion with the Father in your own home. You give thanks for the bread and the wine (or grape juice) representative of the body and the blood of the Lord Jesus Christ, and remind yourself frequently that the loaf of bread has rolled into the camp of your enemies cleansing your household from the impoverishment of the enemy. Believe in the Bread of Life and receive the resurrection power of God in your circumstances. The passages of scriptures related to communion are found in Matthew 26:26–30, Mark 14:22–26, Luke 22:14–20, and I Corinthians 11:24–34.

If your church participates regularly in the sacrament of communion, do so with a renewed understanding as to the power of the body and the blood you hold in your hand. In the Bread of

Life or the body of Christ is everything we need for deliverance from every enemy of righteousness of our soul. Believe it and receive it. There is no more. It is not by our works. It is by our surrender to His work, His sinless life in the flesh, His death on the cross, His burial in the earth, His resurrection from the dead, and His being seated at the right hand of the Father making intercession for us to surrender to Him and believe and receive all He did.

> **Believe in the Bread of Life and receive the resurrection power of God in your circumstances.**

The communion table is the place we become intimate with our heavenly Father and His family. Jesus Christ betrothed us to Him self with His very own body and blood. His very presence meets with us at the Table. Would to God we would come into a renewed understanding that we are bought with a great price. We are betrothed to Another looking forward to the day in which we will one day sit at the table of the marriage supper of the Lamb when our wonderful Lord and Savior and bridegroom, Jesus Christ, the Anointed One, will drink of the cup again when He takes us unto Himself. My prayer is that the Holy Spirit will impart to you a new understanding and zeal to partake of the sacrament of communion with an intimacy of relationship you have never experienced before. *"As often as you do this, do this in remembrance of me."*

Gideon Believed

Gideon believed! He divided his men into three companies of 100 each and gave them all a torch inside a pitcher and a trumpet. They were to smash the pitcher and hold the torch in their left hand and blow the trumpet held in their right hand. Then they were to shout "The sword of the Lord and of Gideon," and stand in their places. This left no chance for the 300 men to even use their swords. The word says the Midianites turned on each other. The Lord delivered Israel out of the hand of the Midianites.

The torch being in their left hand was even significant. The left hand represents being enveloped in darkness. The 300 men held pitchers that contained a torch in darkness. When they smashed the pitchers light suddenly appeared out of the darkness and even in this case the *"Light shines in the darkness, and the darkness did not comprehend it."* (John 1:5) Mass confusion hit the Midian camp and they all began to kill each other when torches of light came out of nowhere and they could not comprehend it.

Resembled the Son of a King
A verse I find very interesting is Judges 8:18. Gideon asked the kings of Midian, Zebah and Zalmunna after the victory against the Midianites, *"What kind of men were they whom you slew at Tabor?"* The kings replied, *"They were like you; each of them resembled the son of a king."* Gideon, because of his surrender to the Lord in the midst of impossible odds, went from being the poorest of the poor and the least of the least of the tribe of Manasseh to one who resembled the son of a king. He was no longer a child or a servant, but a *son*. God is looking for those who will be extraordinary worshippers in the midst of impossible situations walking in extraordinary surrender to Him through whom He can reveal His glory.

Gideon is really a true story. It really happened. There really was an army of Midianites to numerous to count. He believed the word of the Lord and surrendered himself to that word. That is extraordinary surrender. In order for God to do anything supernatural in this earth, He is looking for extraordinary surrender and extraordinary worship from ordinary people who are the poorest of the poor and the least of the least.

Naturally speaking, Gideon was the same as a dead man going against such a vast army with 300 men. Let's bring this down to us today. The cry I hear the most from the body of Christ is, "You just don't know what I am going through. My problems are terrible." The truth is "to each his own." None of our problems are any worse for us than anyone else's problems are for them. We all have challenges that are difficult for us according to our capacity to face them. It feels like we are impoverished by Midianites struggling with life. Gideon was hiding in a winepress threshing his wheat. You may feel like you are in a winepress with pressure on every side struggling with even the necessities of life—putting food on your table etc. But even as the word of the Lord came to Gideon, the word of the Lord is coming to you. He is calling you by your name. He sees who you are. You will come to resemble the son of a king if you will obediently surrender to the voice of the Lord by His grace. It's a process. Everything takes time, but time will pass whether you listen and heed the voice of the Lord or not. The difference is the supernatural results at the end of a life of surrender to the voice of the Lord.

If it had been left up to Gideon, as with all of us, we would have gathered more than 32,000 men to go up against the Midianites. It would not make sense to our natural minds to go up against a multitude with only 300 men. But wait! Let's see what all these numbers represent. This entire story is symbolic of God reaffirming his covenant with His chosen people. Gideon was able to gather to himself 32,000 men from 5 tribes because God had clothed him with Himself and took possession of him causing him to blow a trumpet. It is significant that 32,000 men were gathered from 5 tribes. The number 32 is representative of God's covenant. The number 12 stands for divine authority. The number 20 represents redemption, added together represents God's covenant. The divine authority of God coming through a redeemer will reestablish God's covenant in the land. The number 5 represents grace. Gideon submitted to the divine authority of God surrendering himself to the word of the Lord and allowing the redemptive power of God to be seen in the Land of Israel by His grace. Three is the number that represents resurrection. The 300 men were divided into three groups of 100. We now have the symbol of the trinity—the Father, Son, and Holy Spirit. To allow 32,000 men to fight against the Midianites, as the scriptures say, would have caused Israel to boast of their success. The word says in Zechariah 4:6, *"it is not by might, nor by power but by My spirit says the*

Lord of hosts." When the army was reduced from 32,000 to 300 we find the revelation of the resurrection power of God bringing life out of death to Israel through the work in the Trinity. Talk about using the life of a real man to symbolically reveal a story of Jesus Christ the "One" to come.

Hear the Defeat in the Enemy Camp

You may feel like a dead man with a host against you. I am sure Gideon felt like a dead man until he was told to go into the camp of the Midianites and hear the word of the Lord there. When he heard the defeat in the enemy camp because a loaf of bread rolled in, he worshiped. If we could only hear the defeat being said in the realm of the kingdom of darkness when we as believers truly believe in Jesus Christ being the Bread of Life and that He has rolled into the camp of our enemies and destroy the "Midianites" from our lives, we would worship. He is the light that suddenly appears in our darkness and brings our enemies to mass confusion. It is the resurrection power of God that causes us to rise above the Midianites of our lives.

We say we have faith, but the majority of our faith centers on what we think to be best. Real faith is surrendering ourselves to the Father regardless of the circumstance or the cost with a firm reliance, confident surrender, and a personal trust even when it looks like the odds are innumerable to 300.

Real faith is surrendering ourselves to the Father regardless of the circumstance or the cost with a firm reliance, confident surrender, and a personal trust even when it looks like the odds are innumerable to 300.

All we need is the Father, Son, and Holy Spirit. If we only knew the love the Father has for us and the power of His resurrection. He is looking for people who will not "cut the pipes" and trust Him to bring them out, delivering them and others with them out of the hand of the Midianites. Then we can say with Paul, *"Christ works through me as an instrument in His hands to win obedience from the Gentiles* (those without Christ) *by word and deed, even as my preaching is accompanied with the power of signs and wonders, and all of it by the power of the Holy Spirit."* (Romans 15:18) With Gideon we will resemble the son of a king.

11
Joseph's Crawl Space

Joseph is another interesting character. Joseph is the central character in the majority of the chapters from Genesis 37 to the end of the book of Genesis. His story begins with the declaration that he was his father's favorite. Jacob gave Joseph a coat of many colors and loved him above all of his other children, making all the other kids extremely jealous of Joseph. Joseph had two dreams, and in both dreams, his family members bowed down to him while he reigned over them. He told these dreams to his brothers and his father. His brothers hated him all the more, and his father rebuked him but pondered what Joseph said in his heart.

I've heard some say Joseph was cocky when he told his dreams to his family. I really don't see any reference to arrogance in chapter 37, but what I know is when God gives a dream or a vision and we speak what we have seen to our family and friends, their responses normally are, "You can't do that. You don't have what it takes or the personality to do that. We know you." Some of the comments sound like what Gideon declared about himself, "Why you are the poorest of the poor and the least of the least." I really don't think Joseph was cocky so much as his brother's spoke out of the hardness of their hearts toward him. Joseph didn't pretend to know what the dreams meant. He just spoke what he saw and continued to be faithful and obedient to his father, Jacob.

Jacob sent Joseph to check on his brothers while they were tending the sheep far from home. Joseph's response was. "Here I am." This statement reminds me of Isaiah 6:8, *"Here am I; send me."* Neither father nor son had any idea this was the first day of a journey of destiny toward the realization of Joseph's dreams. When we declare from our heart, "Here am I; send me." We are declaring surrender to the Father's will and our journey to destiny begins. Our problem is we think the journey will be a cake walk, but Joseph's journey was no "cake walk."

His brothers conspired to kill him, but because of Reuben's intercession he was just thrown into a dry, well-like pit. Some Midianites (What is it with these Midianites?) were passing by, so they sold him off as a slave. I can't even imagine the rejection Joseph must have felt as his brothers bargained with the merchants in his hearing. They took Joseph's coat, shredded it, and soaked it in blood from a lamb they killed from dad's flock, making it look like a wild animal got him. This was obviously before the current popular television show CSI and DNA testing. Jacob had no cause not to believe their story. The Midianites sold Joseph in Egypt to Potiphar, who was an officer to Pharoah.

The Lord was with Joseph, and even though he was a slave he was a very successful, prosperous man. Potiphar made Joseph supervisor of his house, and the Lord blessed Potiphar's house because of Joseph. Potiphar's wife decided she would really like to sleep with Joseph. Day after day she propositioned Joseph, but Joseph wouldn't do it saying, *"How can I do this great evil and sin against God?"* (Genesis 39:9) One day in desperation she grabbed his clothes and he fled leaving a piece of his clothes behind. She lied, crying, "Rape!" so Potiphar had Joseph thrown into prison. Sometimes we are thrown into crawl spaces without it being because of anything we have done. Quite frankly, Joseph was acting above reproach but because of a lie he was thrown into prison.

Favor In Prison

The Lord was still with him and showed him mercy and loving kindness and gave him favor in the sight of the warden of the prison. The warden put the charge of the whole prison in Joseph's care and paid no attention to anything that was in Joseph's charge, for the Lord was with him and made whatever he did to prosper. We've seen Joseph in a pit, a slave, and in prison, and he is still a worshipper. God was with him. Never once does the word say Joseph lapsed into self-pity demanding to know why all this was happening to him. Instead I believe he was of the same mind as Paul the apostle determinedly surrendered to God in whatever state he found himself. That catches God's eye.

Pharaoh throws his butler and baker in jail. They land in Joseph's precinct. Both of them have a dream, and Joseph gives the interpretation of their dreams. The butler would be restored to the palace, but the baker would be hanged in three days. He told the butler to remember him to Pharaoh when he was restored to the palace, but the butler was so glad to be alive, he forgot all about Joseph until two years later when Pharoah had a disturbing dream. Suddenly Mr. Butler remembers Joseph.

Pharaoh called Joseph out of the dungeon to stand before him to interpret his dream. Joseph wasn't about to appear before Pharoah like a prisoner. He shaved himself, changed his clothes, and made himself presentable; then he came into Pharaoh's presence.

Pharaoh's dreams spoke of seven years of plenty and seven years of famine. Joseph began to interpret saying, *"God has shown Pharaoh what He is about to do."* (Genesis 41:28) Joseph not only interpreted the two dreams which were really one dream about the same thing, but also gave Pharaoh a solution to the next 14 years of plenty and famine. The plan Joseph laid out seemed good in the eyes of Pharaoh and in the eyes of all his servants. Pharaoh was so impressed with Joseph that this is what he said. *"Forasmuch as your God has shown you all this, there is nobody as intelligent and discreet and understanding and wise as you are. You shall have charge over my house, and all my people shall be governed according to your word with reverence, submission, and obedience. Only in matters of the throne will I be greater than you are. I have set you over all the land of Egypt."* (Genesis 41:39–41) Then Pharaoh took off his signet ring and placed it on Joseph's finger, arrayed him in official vestments, put a gold chain about his neck, and made him to ride in the second limousine.

The Crawl Space

The hand of the Lord was upon Joseph in the midst of his crawl space. In the midst of the darkness of the pit, slavery, and the dungeon the Lord revealed hidden secrets and treasures to Joseph. Then in the fullness of time, God brought him out. God will bring you out of the dark places. What is original with you will release many others. Because of the hidden riches and secrets revealed through Joseph, people were kept alive through the seven years of famine. Preparation was made from the wise counsels of the Lord through Joseph. The time came for Joseph's dreams from so many years before to come to pass. His family came to Egypt for food, not realizing it was Joseph who had become the redeemer of the land in the midst of famine. His brothers did not recognize him after so many years. He no longer looked like the 17 year old kid they had sold to the Midianites. They had cast him into the winter season of his life. In the midst of the deep processing, he was forever changed by the love of God. When spring came and he came out of the crawl space, he didn't look the same. His wisdom and faith was known throughout Egypt. It was God, according to Pharaoh, who had shown Joseph how to redeem the land.

When God brings you out according to Paul in Romans 1:8, the report of your faith will be made known to the world and will be commended everywhere. Joseph's faith was known to the whole world in that day, and it was commended everywhere. He became the redeemer of many. It is said that he is symbolic of Jesus who was to come. In all things he surrendered to the will of the Father knowing that God sees beyond the present conditions to the fulfillment of the destiny that He has placed within our lives.

Don't be moved

Would to God we would not be moved by present conditions or circumstances, but that we would acquire vision that sees beyond how things appear at the moment to God Almighty and His Sovereign will for our life. I doubt if Joseph could have told you when he was 17 years old and had those dreams what the actual reality of those dreams would be. He just continued to walk and stay surrendered to the Father in the midst of whatever circumstance he found himself. That is truly an example of personal trust, confident surrender, and a firm reliance on the Father God. Father really knows best and the best is yet ahead.

Only God Sees the Whole Picture

We see with such finite vision at best. We don't see the whole picture. We don't see how all of us are really fitly joined together to form the holy temple that the Father is building from the beginning of time to the end of time. All of the other ages are a mystery, to us both past and future. We make an idol out of this life and this generation. We tend to believe this generation and the revelation given in this generation is exclusive of all other generations. When in fact, the revelation in this generation builds upon the last and prepares for the next. God is building from age to age, faith to faith, grace to grace, and glory to glory. For us to say it is all about us with no thought to the past or the future is exclusive. God is not about the business of exclusion. He is about the business of inclusion. His inclusion requires an emptying of self and surrendering to His will as He establishes us in our rightful place in this generation in the Holy Temple He is preparing to indwell at the climax of the ages.

God proved through the life of Joseph that if we will continue to seek Him first, everything else will be added unto us. Even in the midst of the dungeon, Joseph found favor and all his needs were met. We can't seek God without learning to worship. We can seek "all these things" and never learn to worship, but we can't seek God without being a worshipper. Worship is what the enemy seeks to steal in the midst of the dark times in our lives. But in the midst of worship and surrender God will give us the treasures and hidden secrets in the darkness, and our faith or our surrender to the Father will be made known in our sphere of influence.

Personally I believe there is a correlation between the darkness and length of time in the crawl space and the sphere of

The Crawl Space

influence of faith when God brings us out into the light. Joseph's sphere of influence reached the uttermost parts of the known world at that time. The weight of the kingdom of Egypt rested upon his shoulders, but history proves he also was in processing 13 years, going from being a slave to the prison dungeons. His freedom was only granted to him by his master or the warden because of God's hand on his life. He could only exit his crawl space experience when God brought him out. He tried to cut the pipes, if you will, when the butler was restored to the kingdom, but the butler forgot him. God kept him under His hand, but when He brought Joseph out of 13 years of processing, he was ready to lead the entire kingdom of Egypt and the other kingdoms of the world because he was surrendered to the Father and dependent upon the grace of God.

When Joseph's father died, his brothers were afraid Joseph would avenge himself for what they had done to him as a child. Joseph replied as a true worshipper of God totally dependent upon Him. Genesis 50:19 says, *"Fear not; for am I in the place of God? As for you, you thought evil against me, but God meant it for good, to bring about that many people should be kept alive, as they are this day. Now therefore, do not be afraid. I will provide for and support you and your little ones. And He comforted them imparting cheer, hope, strength, and spoke to their hearts kindly."*

Redeemer of Many

After 13 years of processing in his life, vengeance had no place in his heart. He viewed all the events in his life as God preparing him for this moment in history. If Joseph would have retained even a seed of bitterness toward his brothers in regards to what they had done to him, history would not have recorded Joseph as the redeemer of many.

The very ones we ridicule and criticize for their visions and dreams, or the ones we condemn for being in tight, dark, difficult places in their natural circumstances, are the very ones who in the days to come could provide spiritual food for us and our little ones. God uses crawl spaces to perfect us into the beautiful instrument He has destined us to be. Crawl spaces are not to punish us, they are to perfect us. If we will only stay under the hand of God in the midst of the crawl space, when He brings us out—even as in Joseph's case—what flows through us will nourish those within our sphere of influence. What flows out of us after a crawl space experience that God has brought us out of is no longer water from the stagnant well of humanity synthetically produced, but it is rivers of living water uniquely original with us. When he brings us out, there is no trace of self-centeredness or a desire for vengeance on our critics. After thirteen years of processing in Joseph's life, he understood that everything that had happened to him was intended by God for good to save many people alive. It was no longer about him, but it was all about the purpose of God in his life. That is the making of a leader of destiny.

> **Crawl spaces are not to punish us, they are to perfect us.**

12
Women Are Emerging From The Crawl Space

It doesn't matter the relationship, the enemy has been intent from the beginning of his fall from heaven on dividing it. He is intent on dividing marriages, friendships, genders, races, and creeds. He hates covenant. The enemy hates the sacrament of marriage so he seeks to divide husband and wife. He then puts division between male and female in any arena he is allowed access or he tempts with unholy relationships between them. He divides races within races. Not only is there division among different colors, but there is also divisions among the same color. There are divisions of creeds or belief systems about methodology of worship. Then there are divisions within each creed causing splits upon splits. How proud the Father must be that all of His children are getting along so well.

Very likely we will all find ourselves in heaven finding out He really didn't care whether we sang fast or slow, with accompaniment or without, prayed from a prayer book, or made the prayer up as we went along. We all know we have personal preference for what we like and what we don't like. God created diversity, not to divide us, but to show *"through the church the complicated, many-sided wisdom of God in all its infinite variety and innumerable aspects might now be made known to the angelic rulers and authorities* (principalities and powers) *in the heavenly sphere."* (Ephesians 3:10) God won't care what color we were or whether we were male or female, Jew or Greek. He created it all and called it good. His question will be, "Did you love one another even as I have loved you in spite of your differences?"

Divisions come because of being focused on ourselves. In

our mind we become the measuring rod all others are measured by. Our opinions are superior in our way of thinking to all other opinions. Whatever color we are, that is the preferred color. Whatever creed we are, that is the "right way." Prejudices are formed in any area of life because of being focused on our self.

I may not enjoy your style of worship but if you are focused on Jesus Christ, the Son of the Living God Who gave Himself for us I can be united with that. If you have surrendered who you are to the Lordship of Christ I can become one with that surrender; however, the truth is our lack of surrender to the Father is what has ultimately divided us. Divisions come because we are focused on our self wanting our own way. We are self-centered instead of Christ-centered. If we continue to be self-centered with our limiting prejudices we will miss what God is doing today.

We are currently living in a day where there is an emergence of women from the darkness of the crawl space into the light in the secular world as well as in the spiritual. I believe there is much significance to this emergence. God is doing a new thing and He may use the unexpected to do it. Here is just some food for thought.

God created the earth and everything in it. When all was good, He created the man, Adam, and put him in the garden He had prepared for him. It was not good for Adam to be alone so God caused a deep sleep to come on Adam. He removed a rib from his side and created the woman Eve. Adam in his original state before Eve was like God in that he contained both male and female, but when God brought Eve into existence, He split Adam removing the female part from him. God's intent was for them to become one even in their separate forms, but the enemy found a way to divide what God intended to walk together in unity.

Compare, Compete, or Complete

Down through history there has been a host of ways the enemy has kept the genders divided. Men have dominated women and women have dominated men in some eras of history. But for the most part historically, women have been kept in "safe" places.

In the western civilization of today we now see women competing in the work place and comparisons are being made of the quality of men versus women in the work place. But competition and comparison just serve to continue the long history of gender division. It isn't a matter of competing and comparing but of completing. God intended both the female and the male parts of Adam to be united as one. They both are distinctly different, and each should be original and complete in Christ. If both male and female are complete in Christ, then they can pour out of that completeness to the other and to their offspring instead of using their energy to get the other to meet their needs.

We have become one flesh physically inside and outside of marriage. The enemy really doesn't mind that. Propagate all the children you want but keep the parents divided spiritually and mentally so only part of Adam is parenting the home. Cause one parent to dominate the other preventing them from being a completed team. That way the children will have a good chance of becoming dysfunctional. If he can divide the home with separation or divorce, so much the better, now he may be able to introduce step-parents who hopefully won't care about the children, or possibly, they will take a perverted interest in the children. The devil really doesn't care about us as parents. We may repent for all of our actions and arrive at our heavenly destination. He is betting he can mess with our kids enough through all our wanderings that they won't repent. We teach more by what we do than what we say.

We teach more by what we do than what we say.

The things we do may not be according to the righteousness of God through Christ Jesus, but they definitely seem like the right thing to do at the time. If it didn't seem like the right thing to do, we would be crazy to do it. That is how subtle sin is. It comes disguised as the right thing to do but in fact it is leading you and your family down a road that leads to death. Proverbs says this very clearly in chapter 14 verse 12. *"There is a way which seems right to a man and appears straight before him, but at the end of it is the way of death."* We must renew our mind to the word of God so that we may prove what is good and acceptable to God, which leads to life.

God's intention was for Adam to have a companion to walk along side of him becoming one with him spiritually, mentally, and physically. When a family has both father and mother in their proper leadership roles, the children are functional and productive in society. Genders weren't intended to dominate or compete with one another. They were meant to complete one another and walk together side by side in all facets of life as they find their completeness in Christ. The male gender, since the advent of Eve, no longer contains the whole of "Adam."

Generally speaking, men are more logical and women are more emotional. This is by no means a deep discourse of the differences between male and female. Suffice it to say that God caused one Adam to become two with the intent that the two Adams would again become one. Male and female united together spiritually, mentally, and physically bring the fullness and completeness God intended to the home.

God gives us the natural to better understand the spiritual. In the family of God, we have been for the most part void of the female voice in leadership. God in this day is emerging strong women in leadership, to come along strong men to cause functionality to come back into the children of God. The church has been dysfunctional. Half of Adam cannot lead in the fullness in which he was created to lead. The enemy knows that and has done everything in his power to keep genders from coming together in the leadership of the home and the church. The women are not to usurp authority over the men. That is not God's intent either. God's intent was for them to walk side-by-side laboring together in all aspects of the home and the church.

There is a sound, original with women, which is beginning to come forth in this day. This sound isn't meant to be a copy of the sound coming from men. Men have developed very well in the sound of their role of Fatherhood. Women are now emerging into the sound of their role of Motherhood in the church. Something we have tended to overlook is that God contains both Fatherhood and Motherhood. There is a female side of God. For example; God is wisdom. Proverbs refers to wisdom in the female gender. God is not a woman as some doctrines would have us to believe. God is greater than one gender. In God are all things. We have robbed the body of Christ by hushing the sound of the Motherhood of God.

You Missed a Spot

The woman reflects the sound of Motherhood coming from the heart of God. The divine understanding of the ancient church in the middle of the third century according to Cyprian of Carthage was "You cannot have God for your Father if you have not the church for your mother." With the emergence of women there is coming a new nurturing sound of motherhood in the church. Generally speaking fathers aren't as particular as to how the children are dressed as mothers are. They aren't as careful about styling their hair or making sure the faces are washed and the teeth are brushed. Men tend to skim over the top while women are more likely to deep clean. Fathers will tell their children to wash up for supper, but mother will look them over and tell them they missed a spot and where it is.

When our children were little sometimes Jerry would help the boys with their clothes. Invariably when Jerry would pull up their britches the center crotch seam would be twisted riding up their left or right hip. Once I said, "Jerry, his pants are on crooked."

He replied, "Well, he can walk can't he?" Yes, our son could walk but with a shorter step on one side. Now women aren't always more particular than men. Men can very definitely be more particular than women. What I am saying is working together they will "see" what perhaps has been hidden from or unnoticed by the other. Together they will complete one another and a new level of excellence will be seen in the body of Christ. The bride of Christ isn't just going to walk but she will walk straight and true. She will be pure, holy, and blameless before her lover and bridegroom, Jesus Christ. He is coming for a church without spot or wrinkle. It is not by accident that women are emerging from the crawl space for such a time as this. We are getting ready for supper—the marriage supper of the Lamb.

One of the main differences in most homes in the role of father and mother that I have observed is the father tends to tell the children what to do following with "because I said so." Fathers are very logical. They don't normally use a lot of words and have little tolerance for instruction. Just do what I say. The theory seems to be if you do what you are told you will figure out the logic behind what you have been told and how to do it as you go along. Mother, on the other hand, generally provides the instruction as to why something is to be done and how to do it. Dad gives the knowledge, and Mom gives the wisdom to back the knowledge. Knowledge is birthed out of logic. Wisdom is birthed out of emotion. Knowledge touches your head assuming all people will respond logically, but wisdom is unassuming and nurtures touching your heart with the truth of knowledge. Together that becomes a beautiful team. God has housed it naturally in two genders. What is exciting is when what is by nature in the genders comes into the supernatural by the Spirit, and that in essence is in the process of happening today.

The emergence of women in ministry today was prophetically announced through Mary, Lazarus's sister, before the death of Jesus. John 12 tells her story.

> *"Six days before the Passover Feast, Jesus came to Bethany, where Lazarus was, who had died and whom He had raised from the dead. So they made Him a supper; and Martha served, but Lazarus was one of those at the table with Him. Mary took a pound of ointment of pure liquid nard (a rare perfume) that was very expensive, and she poured it on Jesus' feet and wiped them with her hair. And the whole house was filled with the fragrance of the perfume. But Judas Iscariot, the one of His disciples who was about to betray Him, said, Why was this perfume not sold for 300 denarii (a year's wages for an ordinary*

workman) *and that* (money) *given to the poor* (the destitute)*? Now he did not say this because he cared for the poor but because he was a thief; and having the bag, the money box, the purse of the Twelve, he took for himself what was put into it* (pilfering the collections*). But Jesus said, Let her alone. It was* (intended) *that she should keep it for the time of My preparation for burial. You always have the poor with you, but you do not always have me."*

Before the death of Jesus a woman stepped forward in the ministry of preparing Jesus' body for burial. She did so despite the criticism from those who would try to steal from the kingdom of God. She did so prophetically of another day when women would be called out to help prepare another body. We are in the last days. It is not by accident that again women are stepping forward to prepare the body. This time the woman is not preparing the body of Christ for burial, but she is helping to prepare the body of Christ for a wedding. She is again stepping out of the obscurity of darkness—out of the crawl space—where she has been in process for such a time as this. She is coming forth with the hidden secrets, riches, and treasures known and found only in the dark places, and from her lips an original sound will come that will be heard by the bride of Christ preparing her for the marriage supper of the lamb.

> **This time the woman is not preparing the body of Christ for burial, but she is helping to prepare the body of Christ for a wedding.**

She is not coming forward to take the place of Fatherhood. She is coming forth to step into the rightful place of Motherhood bringing wholeness back to "Adam." Functionality requires the touch of Father as well as Mother. Both are necessary. Mother is needed for necessary instruction as to how to be the bride and help the bride put on the wedding garment even as Mothers help their daughters put on the wedding gown in preparation for a natural wedding. The theme of ministry now is preparing the offspring for marriage, sowing into them all we are as a Father and a Mother that their lives exceed and excel past all we have ever done—becoming the bride of Christ.

There is a multitude of ladies God is bringing out of dark places into the light. He has been in the process of preparing them all this time. Some are women who have not understood the call of God on their life since there didn't seem to be a place in ministry for them to fit. Seemingly women were unable to do what they felt called to do, which was simply to provide the voice of Motherhood to the body of Christ. But rest assured God has not left the woman out, and He didn't call her by accident. God is bringing her out, and the fruit of her labor along side the labor of the men who are Father's in the faith will be abundantly prosperous in the Kingdom of God. Women will be an integral part in preparing the bride of Christ for the soon coming marriage supper of the lamb.

13
Worship In The Crawl Space

I have written much in this work about worship. Worship is the key to living a surrendered life to God. So what exactly is worship, and how do we do it? One reader, after reading our first book, *"No Time For Goodbyes,"* wrote us a letter regarding the effect of the book on her life.

She said, "The exercise of worship you discussed in your book has helped me overcome depression and loneliness."

I really liked the phrase "The exercise of worship," for worship truly is an exercise. Worship has to be practiced and formed into a habitual way of living. When we say with our mouth simply, "I worship You, Father," we are in affect saying, "Father I declare you to be greater than this moment, whether this moment is good or bad." The word "worship" actually is shortened from an English term "Your Worth-ship" used to address royalty and declaring submission to their authority. To declare my worship to the Father is to declare His worth-ship and Lordship in my life and my submission to His divine authority.

Sometimes we find it easy to worship the Father in the midst of good things. It is easy to thank Him or say, "I worship You," when good is happening in our life; however, sometimes when things are going good, we forget to worship Him. We just take it all for granted and just bask in the goodness we are enjoying with little thought to the Father from whom all things come. Sometimes we become so arrogant as to believe we have created the good life for ourselves, as if God had nothing to do with it when life itself is entirely by His mercy. If we got what we deserved, all of us would have been dead long ago.

In the midst of difficult circumstances, when we say, "I worship You, Father, over whatever the difficulty is presently in my life," we are declaring the Lordship of Christ over the difficulty. When I say, "I worship You over . . ." I am declaring with my mouth that God is greater than . . . and I surrender in worship to His greatness. Worship is the voice of my personal surrender to Him being the Sovereign Lord of my life, and in the midst of whatever the circumstance, I will declare His greatness and Lordship. The enemy hates that and fights hard to prevent us from saying those words. The words, "I worship" declare our personal surrender to the Father, and the enemy wants to keep us in self-centeredness.

> **To declare my worship to the Father is to declare His worth-ship and Lordship in my life and my submission to His divine authority.**

There have been those God has brought to Connie and I who are in a crawl space. We have encouraged them to worship in the midst of the circumstance. Many times the response is, "I can't," or "I'll try, but I can't promise you that I will." The enemy will try to cause our tongues to cleave to the roofs of our mouths or make us choke on the words, "I worship You, Father." He knows that when we begin to worship in the midst of our difficulties we are taking the first step to removing ourselves from the enemy's control and placing ourselves in the hand of the Father. He knows if he cannot prevent us from worshiping, we will eventually become the instrument God has destined us to be. And we wonder why worship is so hard and far removed from us in the midst of difficult circumstances! Worship will bring a new glory into our lives.

In John 4:23-24 Jesus says, *"A time will come, however, indeed it is already here, when the true* (genuine) *worshipers will worship the Father in spirit and in truth* (reality); *for the Father is seeking just such people as these as His worshipers. God is a Spirit* (a spiritual Being) *and those who worship Him must wor-*

ship Him in spirit and in truth (reality)." When scripture is repeated it means "get this!" It is easy to worship the Father in the Spirit when all is going well, but He is also seeking those who will worship Him in the midst of the reality of their living no matter what is going on. We may already be late for work and discover the battery is dead in our car. That is the truth of the reality of living. Will we worship? The Father is seeking just such worshipers.

I have only found two passages of scriptures that speaks of Deity seeking us. The second passage I found is Luke 19:10 which says, *"For the son of Man came to seek and to save that which was lost."* So Deity is seeking two groups of people. The Son is seeking the lost, but once the lost is found the Father is seeking genuine worshipers. The Father is seeking those who will learn to put their complete trust in Him leaning the entirety of their personality on Him and worship Him no matter the circumstance without murmuring or complaining. Worship is the voice of faith and faith is our personal surrender to the Lordship of God Almighty in our lives.

Worship declares the Lordship of Christ over the good and the bad in our life. It is a habit that has to be developed or an exercise that must be cultivated. When we hear good news, we worship God, the giver of all good things. "What a good report! I worship you Father. You are Lord over the good in my life." When we hear a bad report, if we have formed the habit of worship, we will again declare, "I worship You, Father. I declare you to be Lord over this report and I surrender myself to you and your Lordship in my life. I know all things will work together for my good because I love you and I am called according to your purpose for my life so I worship You." If the current situation you are facing has the potential to *break* you, then surrendered in worship to the Father, it has the potential to *make* you. WORSHIP!!!

> **Worship declares the Lordship of Christ over the good and the bad in our life.**

As we worship God in the midst of good and bad, we begin to trust His Lordship. We trust He sees the whole picture of what He is doing with us and our part in the entire scheme of things. Remember Joseph? Can you imagine Joseph taking authority by faith over being sold into slavery and imprisonment? After all, this couldn't be God's will for his life. What did he do to deserve that? Thirteen years of his life was wasted in slavery and prison. What he did to "deserve that" was believe the dreams he had. He worshiped in the midst of his circumstances, declaring the Lordship of God in his life. God never said he would take us out of the midst of the circumstances of life. He said he would walk with us *in* the midst of life and orchestrate the events the enemy means for evil in our life to develop us into His purpose for us. If Joseph would have successfully skirted around all his problems, he would have missed his destiny of saving many people alive in the days of famine.

Oh, you say, God could have skirted him around all the hard stuff and supernaturally landed him next to Pharaoh to accomplish what he was called to do. What kind of man would Joseph have been by Pharaoh's side? That is really a-typical of today. We just want the position. Who cares about the character to support the position? No, it is the processing in the dark that equips, prepares, and produces the quality men and women of God, full of wisdom, discreet in their affairs and full of understanding. God can even use evil events such as being sold into slavery to move us from place to place geographically until we arrive where God wants us to be.

> **True destiny centers upon being processed and perfected into the image that God can use to be a redeemer of others.**

The dream Joseph had of simply seeing his family bowing down to him changed in his understanding. He began to understand the reason was to "save many people alive." Even though God gives us a vision there is much more to the vision that we don't see until we walk through the process. Thank God Joseph worshiped in the midst of the thirteen years of darkness, and his faith and personal surrender to the Father God was made known throughout the world at that time.

If we could only see it is not all about us. God has a plan and a purpose that He has been developing down through all the ages of time. He is using people to fulfill that plan and purpose in their generation. Those who surrender their will to the master plan of God will go through processing. He is after His will and purpose, not our will and purpose. It is the process of the crawl space that actually separates those who will allow their self-centeredness to be removed and become filled with the breath of God from those who won't. God wants to give us kingdom eyes rather than eyes just for earthly things. To declare our worship to Him is to declare, "Not my will but Thine be done." Those who have been history-makers down through the ages didn't have their eyes on their comfort, but they became empty of self and surrendered in worship to the Father. Mary the mother of Jesus said, "Be it unto me according to Thy word," even though she knew she would suffer the disgrace and embarrassment of being pregnant outside of marriage. The angel didn't come to her with Joseph present. She didn't even know how Joseph would take the news, "I'm pregnant." The surrender of our will to the will of the Father is an intimate transaction known only to the Father and us until one day it becomes obvious to those around us. Then people begin to notice there is something different about the person who has surrendered in worship to the Father.

Destiny is Linked to Redemption

Many years ago my husband and I were expecting our first child. We weren't telling people right away. Why I don't know. Usually there is such excitement about having a baby, especially your first, you just have to share the news. I was shopping for groceries and bumped into a good friend of mine. We chitchatted awhile in the parking lot, and suddenly she said, "There is something different about you. You're pregnant aren't you?" Of course,

I couldn't deny. The same thing happens in the spirit. There are those who know us well enough to know there is something different about us almost immediately. You have become pregnant with destiny in the midst of surrender in the crawl space. Others who don't know us as well find out when our destiny has been birthed into the light for all to see.

What I am discovering is destiny is linked to redemption. The destiny God wants to birth through us will somehow work toward the redemption of others who are in our sphere of influence. To fulfill our destiny isn't about living a life centered upon having our own needs met or achieving some level of success that brings honor to us. True destiny centers upon being processed and perfected into the image that God can use to be a redeemer of others. The whole of creation is groaning for the children of God to come into their destinies and redeem the earth from its destruction. *"The creation waits in eager expectation for the sons of God to be revealed. For the creation was subjected to frustration, not by its own choice, but by the will of the one who subjected it, in hope that the creation itself will be liberated from its bondage to decay and be brought into the glorious freedom of the children of God.*" (Romans 8:19–21 NIV)

But It's Dirty Down Here

Many times the dirt or difficulties we have to worship our way through is the same kind of dirt from which we deliver others. God is such an efficient and capable God that He takes what the enemy uses to try to destroy us and orchestrates it to become the most fertile soil in our lives, from which we can redeem countless others.

> **It is not what happens to us, but what happens in us because of what happens to us.**

As we learn to worship God in the midst of life, whatever it is, we give Him opportunity to orchestrate our circumstances to perfect us. It is true that sometimes we find ourselves in the midst of darkness because of our own willfulness. But whether we are there by our own willfulness or because of events beyond our control that had nothing to do with sin (like Joseph, who was beyond reproach and still found himself in darkness), through worship God can take you from where you are to where you are to be in Him. It doesn't matter where you start. What matters is where you end up. What matters is that we end up in true surrender to The Sovereignty of The Most High God in worship.

> **Those who learn the art of worship open the door for the grace (power and ability) of God to intervene in their behalf and turn everything the enemy meant for evil to good for those who love God (worship God) and who are called according to His purpose.**

Just saying, "I worship" when we don't know what else to do or when we don't know what else to say, allows God to come on the scene. Just saying, "I worship" gives God the divine authority in our life and takes power away from the enemy. It is not what happens to us, but what happens in us because of what happens to us. Worshiping, regardless of what has happened to us, allows the Father to work in us. *"Not in your own strength, for it is God Who is all the while effectually at work in you* (energizing and creating in you the power and desire), *both to will and to work for His good pleasure and satisfaction and delights."* (Philippians 2:13)

The reason we don't surrender completely and totally to the Father is we really don't trust that He knows and has the best for us. We don't believe He has our best interest in mind. When we begin to go through a hard time, all we see is the hard time. We can't see in our finiteness what God has in mind unless we stay under His hand allowing Him to bring us out of the crawl space.

But you argue, "If I don't take authority over the bad

things that come, the enemy will defeat me and destroy me. There has to be more to it than worship." Worship takes the bad things that come and allows God to turn them into good things for His kingdom, producing an eternal weight of glory in us. Bad things as well as good things are going to come. None of us can escape shear facts of life. The key to all things whether good or bad is worship. Worship is a habitual exercise. Those who learn the art of worship open the door for the grace (power and ability) of God to intervene in their behalf and turn everything the enemy meant for evil to good for those who love God (worship God) and who are called according to His purpose. (Romans 8:28)

There are those who will never hear the call of the purpose of God in their lives, even though as we read earlier in Ecclesiastes that God has put a divine purpose in all of us that can only be satisfied by God. They will be so self-centered that to see anything beyond what is affecting them at the moment is out of the question. To hear the call of the purpose of God in your life, you must have vision to see beyond the present to the Father who knows your purpose and is the only one capable of using events of life to orchestrate that destiny within us.

So like the words to a song that God gave me in the midst of my crawl space:

> *"I may not know what to do,*
> *But my eyes are on You, and I worship You.*
> *I may not know what to say*
> *As I walk through each day, but I worship You.*
> *It's Your face that I seek. In myself I am weak,*
> *but I worship You. I worship You.*
>
> *When nothing seems to go right*
> *And there's no end in sight, I worship You.*
> *When my trials seem long*
> *And my heart has lost its song I will worship You.*
> *In the midst of everything, this sacrifice I bring.*
> *I worship You, I worship You.*

As I worship nothing else seems to matter.
In your presence is such peace all fear is shattered.
As I worship we come into our secret place
And you touch me deep within as we are face to face.

You teach me to say
Regardless of my day 'I worship You.'
In good times or bad
When I'm happy or when I'm sad, I will worship You.
So no matter how I feel,
The faith that is real will worship You.
    So I worship You."

Faith is our personal surrender to a Sovereign Lord, and worship is the voice of that surrender. Faith can either be concentrated on our own needs being met, or it can be about us surrendering to the process needed to make us the history-maker we were destined to be. Surrendered faith will cause us to be an instrument of redemption in our sphere of influence in the earth, and in the process, all of our personal needs will also be met according to His riches in Christ Jesus.

I am reminded of all the times I have begun to search for something I was in need of at the moment. In the process, I discovered other items that I had given up ever finding. Not only was I able to find the item I needed for the moment, but I was blessed with the discovery of other items that seemed lost forever and completely out of my reach. Somehow that is how it works in the Kingdom of God. If we will seek first and foremost His Kingdom—His presence—then in pursuit of His presence, we will find along the way everything else we have been looking for and hoping to find. Those things were not the goal of our search, but they were wonderful benefits discovered along the way

> **Faith is our personal surrender to a Sovereign Lord, and worship is the voice of that surrender.**

toward the goal of our search. The promise remains, *"for you who seek first the kingdom of God and His righteousness, all these things will be added unto you."* (Matthew 6:33) But what does it mean to seek the Kingdom of God and His righteousness?

14
"Seek Ye First Kingdom Of God" In The Crawl Space

"One thing I have asked of the Lord, that will I seek, inquire for and insistently require; that I may dwell in the house of the Lord in His presence all the days of my life, to behold and gaze upon the beauty (the sweet attractiveness and the delightful loveliness) of the Lord and to mediate, consider, and inquire in His temple. For in the day of trouble He will hide me in His shelter; in the secret place of His tent will He hide me; He will set me high upon a rock. You have said, Seek My face (inquire for and require My presence as your vital need). *My heart says to You, Your face* (Your presence), *Lord, will I seek, inquire for, and required* (of necessity and on the authority of Your Word)." (Psalm 27:4, 5, & 8) David knew what it meant to seek the kingdom of God.

"The Kingdom of God is not a matter of (getting the) *food and drink* (one likes)*, but instead it is righteousness* (that state which makes a person acceptable to God) *and* (heart) *peace and joy in the Holy Spirit."* (Romans 14:17) The Kingdom of God is found only in seeking His presence. Zephaniah 2:3 echoes this same thought. *"Seek the Lord* (inquire for Him, inquire of Him and require Him as the foremost necessity of you life), *all you humble of the land who have acted in compliance with His revealed will and His commandments; seek righteousness, seek humility* (inquire for them, require them as vital). *It may be you will be hidden in the day of the Lord's anger."*

Vital Necessity

I remember when the Lord began to speak to me on this

passage and the natural example He gave me as to what "requiring the Lord as the vital and foremost necessity of our life" could be compared. My mother-in-law, who has since passed on to be with Jesus, was on kidney dialysis. In order for her to live, she had to have her blood purified of all toxins that the kidneys were unable to remove independently of assistance. The quality and longevity of her life would not afford her the luxury of missing the scheduled dialysis times. It was the first thing on her calendar of events. Life for mom and dad revolved around that scheduled 4 - 5 hours three times a week or more, depending on how well they were able to remove the fluid and toxic build up each day. Dialysis wasn't something they would tend to if they got around to it. It was the thing they took care of first, and everything else would take second place and only be taken care of if they got around to it.

To require something as the foremost necessity of your life, in essence means your life revolves around the thing required. To seek first the kingdom of God, simply is saying, "My life revolves around seeking the Presence of the Most High God." Even as David suggests, "I want to behold and gaze upon the beauty of the Lord. I want to know for myself His attractiveness and His delightful loveliness. I want to meditate on Him and consider Him and inquire Him in His temple." In other words, I want an intimate relationship with the Most High God. I don't want to know about Him. I want to know Him, and I know Him by requiring that my life revolve around Him. This intimacy isn't achieved in an attitude of I will talk to God and read my Bible when I can get around to it.

For many the sum total of their experience with God is reading a few words from the Bible or a devotional and praying a prayer of blessing and protection once in a while or perhaps daily. This is cold and lifeless. If we were to listen to our hearts, we would know this isn't fulfilling. So we busy ourselves throughout our lives trying to find that which fulfills yet never achieving. Our hearts are crying out for that intimate relationship David describes. That kind of relationship with the Father isn't for a select few. It is for all who will seek first the kingdom or the presence of God. Matthew 7 says, *"Seek and you will find."*

When my husband died, I was surrounded with all the things he had provided for the children and me. We had enjoyed a good life, and our needs and even our wants for the most part had been attained. Everything I owned was representative of a day when I had my husband's presence. Now I had his *presents* but not his *presence.* If we are not careful, we will turn our attention to the hand of God and His provision, rather than the face of God and His presence. We will begin to seek things to fill what we feel we are lacking in our physical lives when God wants us to seek His presence, and in the process, you will find all you need provided along the way.

I Shall Not Want

After Jerry died, there was a great void and sense of loss and lack. Lack demands a response of "seeking." The question we have to answer is, "Where will we seek to fill the lack?" The word admonishes us to seek the Kingdom of God first. The enemy wants us to seek out our own solution based out of our own thinking to fill the lack. This leads to death. The way that leads to life is seeking the kingdom of God or seeking His presence. He wants to make us so complete in Him that we have no lack according to Colossians 1:28. Psalm 23:10 says in essence that God wants to fill us so full of Himself that we become a whole person fully satisfied in His presence.

> **Lack demands a response of "seeking."**

After more than two years, I am still a widow. My natural circumstances have not changed, but what has changed is the presence of God within me. I have discovered I am complete in Him. I may be a widow in the natural, but I am the bride of Christ in the spiritual. The peace in this place is beyond my understanding. To the natural mind, it seems impossible to think that there could be peace and fulfillment in being single. But oh there is! It comes by pressing into the spirit and seeking first the presence of God to fill the lack felt in our physical circumstances.

For too long we have filled the lack in our physical circumstances with what we think is best by physical means. We rush out and replace whatever it is we have lost as quickly as possible. But a physical lack gives opportunity to fill ourselves with the Spirit of the Living God, allowing Him to make us complete, and He will do just that. He is waiting for vessels that will surrender to His presence in the midst of whatever the lack is in their lives. That is difficult to do. We want the problem fixed yesterday. We don't like problems. Problems hassle with our convenience and our stability. Quite frankly, for the most part, we can be defined as a people of convenience, becoming unstable in the midst of the storms of life. We are easily shaken and disturbed when difficulties arise. The first question foremost on our mind is, "What am I going to do?" Those of us who are truly walking in Matthew 6:33 will "seek first the kingdom" by worshiping the Father in the midst of the difficulty and finding His presence in the midst of the storm. Those of us, who are only seeking things, will seek to fix the problem ourselves.

Our faith (or who we surrender to) is told by what we seek in the face of lack. Remember, faith is our personal surrender. Ask yourself this question. "In the midst of a storm, who or what do I surrender to or seek first? Do I surrender myself in worship to the Most High God seeking His presence in the midst of this storm and wait patiently, or do I surrender to my own mind or the mind of others seeking a quick fix by drawing my own conclusion as to what I should do in the midst of the storm?" If our attitude is it is easier to sin and get forgiveness, we are surrendered to the law of the flesh. If our attitude is I am going to stay under the hand of God until he brings me through in His righteousness, we are surrendered to the Law of the

> **Our faith (or who we surrender to) is told by what we seek in the face of lack.**

Spirit of Life. Our answer will prove to us in whom or what our faith is, as well as around whom or what our life is revolving. We'll find our faith or surrender to be either to our ability and self-centeredness, or to God's ability and His presence. It is always one or the other.

Again We Worship

As we worship, we allow the grace or the power and ability of God to come on the scene in the midst of the storm and do what we could never do. Worship releases His ability to go to work in our lives. We release ourselves from being motivated by self to hearing wisdom from the Holy Spirit. In worship, we release the heavenly Father to direct our steps and show us the way to go. Psalm 16:11 says, *"You will show me the path of life; in Your presence is fullness of joy, at Your right hand there are pleasures forevermore."* In the presence of the God almighty, in our secret place with Him, we can be sheltered in the peace of God and strengthened in our inner man no matter what is happening to our outer man. Paul says in II Corinthians 4:16–18, *"Therefore we do not become discouraged* (utterly spiritless, exhausted, and wearied out through fear). *Though our outer man is* (progressively) *decaying and wasting away, yet our inner self is being* (progressively) *renewed day after day. For our light, momentary affliction* (this slight distress of the passing hour) *is ever more and more abundantly preparing and producing and achieving for us an everlasting weight of glory* (beyond all measure, excessively surpassing all comparisons and all calculations, a vast and transcendent glory and blessedness never to cease!) *Since we consider and look not to the things that are seen but to the things that are unseen; for the things that are visible are temporal* (brief and fleeting), *but the things that are invisible are deathless and everlasting."*

> **Worship releases His ability to go to work in our lives.**

If we could only see our crawl space experiences and storms of life as Paul puts it as "only light and momentary afflictions" with a purpose. They produce and achieve in us the glory of God. He ends with saying to seek the invisible. Seek the presence of God. That is deathless and everlasting. Things are here today and gone tomorrow. Nothing pleases the Father more than for His children to seek His presence as the foremost necessity in their life.

15
"And Seek His Righteousness" In The Crawl Space

By Vine's Expository Dictionary of New Testament Words righteousness is said to be:

"The character or quality of being right or just; it was formerly spelled 'rightwiseness,' which clearly expresses the meaning. It is used to denote an attribute of God, e.g., Rom. 3:25, 26 the context of which shows that "the righteousness of God" means essentially the same as His faithfulness, or truthfulness, that which is consistent with His own nature and promises. Rom. 3:2,26 speaks of His righteousness as exhibited in the Death of Christ, which is sufficient to show men that God is neither indifferent to sin nor regards it lightly. On the contrary, it demonstrates that quality of holiness in Him, which must find expression in His condemnation of sin.

Righteousness is that gracious gift of God to men whereby all who believe on the Lord Jesus Christ are brought into right relationship with God. This righteousness is unattainable by obedience to any law, or by any merit of man's own, or any other condition than that of faith in Christ. The man who trusts in Christ becomes 'the righteousness of God in Him.' Faith thus exercised brings the soul into vital union with God in Christ, and inevitably produces righteousness of life, that is, conformity to the will of God."

We are told in Matthew 6:33 to "seek His righteousness." The definition I have always used and been taught was simply "right standing with God." We gained that right standing with God because the blood of Jesus covered our sins. This is all very true, but if we are seeking God's Kingdom or His presence and we are seeking His righteousness, our seeking should lead us somewhere. Our seeking should lead us to growth in righteousness. To seek righteousness by faith inevitably produces righteousness of life or conformity to the will of God according to Vine's Expository Dictionary.

The crawl space is meant to cause us to dig deeper into His presence, His kingdom, and His righteousness and mature in reliance upon Him. If we have a patterned "Sin/Repent" mentality, instead of staying in the process of maturing and trusting God to bring us through, we will opt out of the crawl space. Seldom do we lean into the grace of God that will keep us in the midst of the crawl space and will cause growth and maturity in our lives. It is much easier to just exit the crawl space by our own effort, *"cut the pipes,"* repent for the sin we find ourselves in due to our premature exit, cry out for His mercy, and continue on in the same childishness, instead of growing from faith to faith, grace to grace, and glory to glory, becoming the mature bride of Christ.

God is a God of growth. Throughout the scriptures, He uses examples of growth. Even the parable of the rich master that gave his servants talents of silver to invest while he was gone, shows growth being commended.

God is a God of growth.

Two of servants doubled the talents they were given, but the last servant hid the talent he was given. The profitable servants were commended, but the one who produced no growth was thrown into outer darkness. (Matthew 25:30) Paul says in Romans 1:17, *"In the Gospel a righteousness which God ascribes is revealed, both springing from faith and leading to faith* (disclosed through the way of faith that arouses to more faith). *As it is written, the man who through faith is just and upright shall live and shall live by faith."* The righteousness God ascribes leads from faith to faith, grace to grace, and glory to glory. God is a God of growth.

In our minds it seems we have been put off from the idea

of ever becoming righteous. We have settled for a concept that all of us will sin—probably everyday, but we can ask for forgiveness. Then, the blood of Jesus will cover our sin causing us to be in right standing with God. He can look at us through the blood of Jesus. This concept and use of the blood of Jesus reduces the effect of His blood sacrifice to be no more than the blood of bulls and goats slaughtered day after day and year after year before Christ died for our sin, making a sacrifice once and for all. The blood of bulls and goats covered sin until the next time we sinned, and then we would cover our sin again. The blood of Jesus has the power to deliver us from sin's dominion, so it will no longer have a hold on us.

> **Seek after conformity to God's revealed will, in thought, deed, and purpose, empowered by faith in the grace of God through the blood of Jesus.**

What does it mean to seek His righteousness? It actually means to seek after conformity to God's revealed will, in thought, deed, and purpose, empowered by faith in the grace of God through the blood of Jesus. We all know in our own strength we can't live up to what God ascribed righteousness to be according to the Law. We all know we fell miserably short. Paul says it so accurately in Romans 7:18, 24–25. *"I know that nothing good dwells within me, that is in my flesh. I can will what is right, but I cannot perform it, I have the intention and urge to do what is right, but no power to carry it out. O unhappy and pitiable and wretched man that I am! Who will release and deliver me from the shackles of this body of death? I thank God that He will deliver me through Jesus Christ the Anointed One our Lord! So then indeed I of myself with the mind and heart, serve the Law of God, but with the flesh the law of sin."*

In our flesh we are powerless to be righteous and uphold the Law, which is the revealed will that God ascribes righteousness to be. But through the blood of Jesus that cleanses us from all unrighteousness, we grow into the righteousness that God ascribes. This growth comes by seeking His righteousness that leads to conformity to His righteousness. As we read the New Testament, the Fathers of the early church since the death of Jesus ascribe the concept that we are made righteous by grace through faith in the shed blood of Christ the Anointed One, and *IF* we sin, we have an advocate with the Father. The concept of the scriptures is sin is to be the exception, not the rule.

"My little children, I write you these things so that you may not violate God's law and sin, but if any should sin, we have an Advocate (One Who will intercede for us) with the Father—it is Jesus Christ the all righteous (upright, just, Who conforms to the Father's will in every purpose, thought, and action). And He is the propitiation for our sins and not for ours alone but also for the whole world. And this is how we may discern (daily, by experience) that we are coming to know Him (to perceive, recognize, understand and become better acquainted with Him); if we keep (bear in mind, observe practice) His teachings (precepts, commandments). Whoever says, I know Him (I perceive, recognize, understand) and am acquainted with Him but fails to keep and obey His commandments (teachings) is a liar, and the truth (of the Gospel) is not in him. But he who keeps (treasures) His Word (who bears in mind His precepts, who observes His message in its entirety) truly in him has the love of and for God been perfected (completed, reached maturity). By this we may perceive (know, recognize, and be sure) that we are in Him. (I John 2:1–5 AMP)

The blood of Christ is not to be used as the blood of bulls and goats. The truth of the Gospel is the blood of Jesus cleanses us from sin. It doesn't roll sin forward or cover sin like the blood of bulls and goats. The blood of Jesus removes sin from us, eliminating the desire by grace though faith. We have the concept today that since we couldn't keep the Law, Christ came and did away with the Law, so that we no longer have to uphold or confirm the Law in our lifestyle. His blood will cover us anyway, so we can be righteous before God. However, Matthew 5:17 says this, *"Do not think that I have come to do away with or undo the Law or the Prophets; I have come not to do away with or undo but to complete and fulfill them."* He didn't do away with the Prophets. He fulfilled every word that had been spoken by the Prophets regarding Him. He didn't come to undo the Law, so that God's grace would just let us remain in our sin. He was the only one that ever lived who fulfilled the Law in all respects, never breaking it and living up to the righteousness ascribed by God, and He did it as a man dependent upon the grace of God. John 1:14 says, *"He was full of grace and truth."* The 16th verse goes on to say, *"Out of His fullness we have all received."* Then in Romans 8:29 it is stated, *"For those whom He foreknew* (of whom He was aware and loved beforehand), *He also destined from the beginning* (foreordaining them) *to be molded into the image of His Son* (and share inwardly His likeness*), that He might become the firstborn among many brethren."* Being the firstborn of many means we can follow his lead and share inwardly his likeness.

Jesus did not come to do away with the Law nor undo the Law. He came to give us the grace and truth to be conformed to His likeness. By grace, through faith, in His blood he delivered us from sin's dominion, so that sin would no longer have a hold on us. He came to be that Bread of Life that will roll into the camp of the enemies of righteousness in our souls, destroying their camp. He came to do for us what we could not do ourselves.

God still condemns sin in the flesh. He gave us the Law through Moses, but all that did was expose more sin as the enemy used the Law as a weapon against us according to Romans 7:9–11. God instituted the blood sacrifice of bulls and goats so He could tolerate our sin by looking at it through an animal's blood. But there was coming a day in the fullness of time in which God the Son would become incarnate or God in the flesh as the son of man. The son of man fulfilled the Law. He kept it! He never disobeyed any part of the Law. He was the sinless sacrifice. He did what none of the rest of us could ever do in our weakened flesh. With the life, death, burial, and resurrection of the sinless son of man, God gave us the solution to our not being able to keep the Law and walk in righteousness before Him. *"God has done what the Law of God could not do,* (its power) *being weakened by the flesh* (the entire nature of man without the Holy Spirit.) *Sending His own Son in the guise of sinful flesh and as an offering for sin,* (God) *condemned sin in the flesh* (subdued, overcame deprived it of its power over us because we accept that sacrifice). (Romans 8:3) He didn't do away with the Law. He made a way to keep the Law. By grace (God's power and ability), through faith (personal surrender), in the blood of Jesus we are daily delivered from sin's dominion. We can actually live a life controlled by the Spirit instead of controlled by the flesh. Faith in Christ the Anointed One made that possible. *"Now I am discharged from the Law, having died to what once restrained and held me captive. Now I serve not under obedience to the old code of written regulations but under obedience to the prompting of the Spirit in newness of life."* (Romans 7:6) Actually the Spirit keeps us in check according to the precepts of the Law better than the written Law was able to do.

If we are being led by the Spirit of God and seeking His righteousness, when we even begin to think down a road that is against the righteousness of God, the Holy Spirit will rise up within us and red flag our thoughts. If we

Actually, we spend more time and effort believing for a car that will take us around the block than we do in seeking His righteousness that will take us all the way home.

continue when the Holy Spirit has checked us in our spirit, we are choosing to walk after the flesh and the dictates of the flesh. It is only by leaning into the grace of God by faith in the blood of Jesus that we will be able to make the right choice and not act according to what the flesh wants.

We say everyone has to sin a little everyday because we simply do not want to use our faith in the grace of God to overcome the test that is before us. It wouldn't be a good temptation if it wasn't pleasing to our flesh. We use our faith for things. We also need to use our faith to walk in the righteousness of God through Christ Jesus. Actually, we spend more time and effort believing for a car that will take us around the block than we do in seeking His righteousness that will take us all the way home.

Paul makes it very clear throughout the book of Romans, our flesh, sin nature, or to put it another way, self-centeredness, is to have died with Christ. *"My old unrenewed self* (self-centeredness) *was nailed to the cross with Him in order that my body of sin might be made ineffective and inactive for evil, that I might no longer be a slave of sin. For when a man dies, he is freed from the power of sin among men."* (Romans 6:6–7) We could not keep the Law in our flesh, but God gave us the way to live through Jesus Christ, controlled by the Spirit and not controlled by the lust of the flesh.

> **Anything less than depending upon the grace of God through faith in His blood is living by our own righteousness.**

So what does it mean to really seek His righteousness? It is to surrender my desire to live after the dictates of my flesh to the Father. *"If I continue in my self-centeredness, living after the dictates of my flesh, I will surely die. But if through the power of the Holy Spirit, I am habitually putting to death* (making extinct, deadening) *the evil deeds prompted by the body, I will* (really and genuinely) *live forever."* (Romans 8:13)

We cannot put our flesh or evil desires to death by our own will power or righteousness. Oh, sometimes we can change or modify our behavior, but that affords us the opportunity to boast about what we have been able to accomplish. God is not interested in what we can accomplish. He is interested in our surrender to His will and allowing His grace to bring it to pass in our lives. Anything less than depending upon the grace of God through faith in His blood is living by our own righteousness. Seeking God's righteousness is declaring my total dependence upon the grace of God to change me, delivering me step by step, day by day out of darkness (being controlled by the flesh) in every area of my life into His marvelous light (being controlled by the Spirit).

We appropriate the grace of God by crying out for it. By just speaking the words, "Grace, Father, grace," we are allowing God's power to come on the scene of our weakness. *"Let us then fearlessly and confidently and boldly draw near to the throne of grace* (the throne of God's unmerited favor, power, and ability to us sinners)*, that we may receive mercy* (for our failures) *and find grace to help in good time for every need* (appropriate help and well-timed help, coming just when we need it). (Hebrews 4:16) The Spirit of God within us will instruct us if we will just pay attention to His prompting. It is better to live in the power and ability of God's grace to prevent us from sinning than need His mercy after we have sinned.

"Rightwiseness" according to the Vine's was the original spelling of righteousness. Walking rightly and wisely, conforming to the faithfulness and truthfulness of God in nature and character, and it is achieved only by grace through faith in the blood of Jesus.

We have sold righteousness and grace too short. We have diluted the message of both, and we have now produced a generation who is living up to the lowest tolerance according to the message we have taught. The message of grace that has come through to the lay person and leaders alike is that grace covers my sin allowing me to live in unrighteousness while God winks at my unrighteousness and gives me divine favor regardless, no matter what I do or how I live. Our message in regards to righteousness that has come through to lay people, is when we sin (and we will sin every day if not multiple times a day) we just need to be quick to ask God to forgive us each time. So we do the same things over and over, and God is obligated by the blood of Jesus to allow us to stand in righteousness before Him. Nothing in this kind of teaching encourages maturity in Christ. This kind of teaching encourages playing just inside the door of salvation, never growing in conformity to the righteousness of God.

One day I heard the Lord say in my spirit, "I am not coming back for a child bride." The earth and its crawl spaces are to grow us up to become mature in the faith. When He comes to receive His bride to Himself, *"He is coming for a glorious church without spot or wrinkle, washed in the blood of the lamb and walking in serene peace free from fear and agitating passions."* (2 Peter 3:14) Psychologists tell us when single people begin to look for a mate; they choose people of similar beauty, character, values, and interests—another "natural" given to better understand the "spiritual." When Christ returns to receive His bride, she will have gazed into His beauty while seeking His presence until her beauty reflects that of His. She will have stayed under the hand of God in the midst of hard, dark circumstances until she emerges, walking in the integrity and character of God. In seeking His righteousness, her values will have conformed to His. And interests—one thing have I desired and that is to dwell in the presence of the Christ the Anointed One forever.

16
Becoming An Instrument In The Crawl Space

In days of old The Father would ask the prophet, "What do you see?" That question was asked of me, and this is what I saw. I saw a tree in full foliage, full of life with limbs swaying in the wind. Sound came from the tree as the leaves were moved by the wind. Birds sat upon its branches, and there was a cool breeze beneath its shade. But in the dark of night, a severe storm came. In the darkness of night, the wind blew with such force the tree bowed low. By morning the wind ceased, all became still, and the tree righted itself. In the light of morning, it was discovered there were branches fallen upon the ground. A variety of responses came from the remaining living branches still connected to the tree and also from the dying branches upon the ground.

The living branches swaying again in the gentle wind of the new day began to sing, "We are so glad we are not as one of them who lay dying upon the ground." Within the chorus, the individual sound of pity could be heard. "We're so sorry for you. Oh you poor dear, what you must be going through." Other limbs began to counsel. "If you would have prayed more or read your Bible more and had more faith, nothing would have happened to you of this sort. You would have weathered the storm and still be connected like me."

Other limbs passed judgment upon those lying on the ground. "You must have committed a great sin, and that has cast you down. Where have you opened the door to the enemy to allow him to attack you like this?"

The response from the dying branches lying on the ground was equally as noisy. Most were murmuring and complaining.

"We are still full of green foliage and fruit lying here upon the ground. Why is this happening to us? We were alive and well connected to the tree. Why us? Why me? This can't be happening to me!"

Yet others are caught up in hindsight. "If only I would have . . . I should have . . . Why didn't I . . . ?"

Still other limbs lashed out in rage, "It was that branch next to me. It is all his fault. He is the reason I am dying here upon the ground. And God! Where were You? You've let me down! If this is the way You are I don't want any part of You."

But in the midst of the branches slowly dying on the ground lay "One" trembling in weakness. Quietly escaping from his lips was heard the sound of surrender. "Father, help me! I don't understand why I have been broken off the tree, but I worship You in the midst of this death. Everything is getting dark, but I will keep my eyes on You."

As with all things, in the process of time, the foliage representative of a fruitful day, dried up from the limbs on the ground and they withered away. The limbs were dry and hardened in the position in which they fell. The limbs who murmured and complained in their self-centeredness and arrogance continued on their path of death until one day they were scooped up and thrown into the fire as kindling. But something strange and wonderful was taking place in "One." The crooked places in his limb were becoming straight as hardness came to his frame. "One" continued to worship in the midst of his pain and suffering in the dark. He remained patient and steadfast in the midst of his death upon the ground.

When the fullness of time had come, "One" was chosen by the Master. The Master took "One" in His hand and began another process of change. Again, "One" did not comprehend but continued steadfast and patient, worshiping in the touch of the Master's hand. The Master began to bore clean through "One" from one end to the other until there was nothing left of "One" but a hollow shell. "One" had become totally empty of self. The process was painful and hard to endure, but "One" kept his eyes on the Master, trusting His hand and in Him was secure.

Then the Master began to bore more holes in various places. With each new hole there was less of "One." "One" still could not comprehend, but "One" continued to keep his eyes on the Master, and from his lips came precious words. "I don't understand what is happening to me, but I surrender to you and I worship you. You are all I desire. Fill me with Yourself."

The Master began to sand and sand until "One" was completely smooth. Then He polished "One" with a protective coat that caused a beautiful glow. But "One's" body remained lifeless from the death he had sustained until the Master brought "One" to His face and kissed him with the kisses of His mouth and filled Him with His breath. Placing His fingers upon the holes, suddenly was heard a brand new sound. This sound was distinctly different from the rustling of the leaves in the tree. It was the sound played by the Master's breath through the instrument of "One." "One" no longer played in the wind with the other limbs of the tree, but "One" became the message to be heard as the breath of God played through him. "One" is no longer blown about by circumstances responding to the wind like all the other limbs in the tree, but "One" has become stable in serene peace moved only by the hand of God, and the sounds issuing forth from "One" begin only with the breath of God.

> **"One" is no longer blown about by circumstances responding to the wind like all the other limbs in the tree, but "One" has become stable in serene peace moved only by the hand of God, and the sounds issuing forth from "One" begin only with the breath of God.**

The destiny within us will never be developed while we are dancing in the soft south wind in the light. We are developed in the darkness of night, in the constricted places that are hard to

The Crawl Space

deal with and hard to bear. Sometimes it feels like we have been cut off and there is no hope. There is a dying that leads to death—eternal death; but there is also a dying that leads to life—the resurrected life of God issuing from our being.

As long as the wind is softly stirring and everything is green and good in our lives, it doesn't give an accurate picture of the type of people we are in our inner being. But when the storms of life come, it reveals who we really are. If we will surrender who we are to the Father, He will make us into the instrument we were created to be. Storms come to all of us at some point in time in our lives. They are a fact of life. The storm can come in the form of a bad marriage, wayward children, death of a loved one, bankruptcy etc. etc.

People not currently affected by a storm can be judgmental or critical of those in the midst of a crisis situation. We would be a lot less apt to criticize if we only understood what the end result could be under the hand of God. The enemy wants us to judge and criticize. His plan for those fallen from a storm is to make kindling out of them. Our judgment and criticism can help his plan along quite nicely. God's plan for those fallen in a storm is to make them inwardly into His image. He is after complete and total dependency and surrender to Him so He can develop them into who they were destined to be.

In the midst and wake of a major storm, there is major change. As long as we are attached to the tree, we are well able to produce foliage. It is easy to slip into a self-righteous mode, and we all sound alike blowing in the wind responding to the external circumstances. But when God wants to produce a new sound, things shake up a bit to cause us to become an instrument in His hand. He uses the process of life to do it.

Sounds Abound

God does a new thing in us, actually in answer to our own cry. From some of the limbs swaying in the wind in the midst of the foliage, a quiet groan begins to stir from their heart, "Use me." A seed of destiny that was placed within them by God is now in the fullness of time. Events must come to rid us of self-centeredness in order for His glory to be revealed in our destiny. If you can accomplish the destiny God has placed within you, I question if it truly was God-given. If you can accomplish the vision, then you were successful at manipulating resources, but your vision will die with you. God's destiny in us is always beyond us, so man cannot boast.

When God finds a "limb" of the tree in the fullness of time and the cry is coming from within them, "Be it unto me according to thy word," the Holy Spirit begins to hover just like He hovered over Mary the mother of Jesus. Many times the limb is then subjected to criticism and embarrassment, assessed by onlookers with all manner of opinions. If Joseph had not stood by Mary's side, she would have been stoned. All this is to rid us of self-centeredness. It wasn't about Mary. It was about the seed that was within her that would be produced by the breath of God to be The Redeemer.

When God brings us out of the crawl space the destiny birthed from our lives will reveal a new facet of the beauty of God. There will be a new strength resembling a "Mighty Warrior" even as Gideon, a redeemer of many. Somehow in the midst of the darkness, it stops being about the success we will have in fulfilling our destiny, and it becomes about God filling us with Himself. Circumcision comes to our heart as we desire the praise of God, the very breath that He breathes in us, more than the praise of men.

A Change in the Weather

Life is ebb and flow. Both are normal to life. All of nature ebbs and flows. Sometimes it's high tide, and sometimes it's low tide. Sometimes it is winter; sometimes it's spring. All of life is a cycle. We have learned to adapt to the natural cycles of life or changes of the seasons, but the spiritual cycles of life is another thing. Spiritually we believe we should be in a perpetual springtime and harvest. The truth is we also experience scorching heat and blistering cold spiritually. The difference is all who live in the

The Crawl Space

same town, going through the same physical weather changes at the same time have something to talk about. "My, isn't it cold today! I sure hope this cold snap turns soon. I'm ready for some warmer days." Spiritually, we live in different weather zones. Of course that gives us something to talk about also.

Others may be in sunshiny Florida with oranges heavy on the trees while we are in the heat of the Sahara Desert or in the frigid cold of the North Pole with no vegetation or fruit in sight. While some of us are in full fruit production, others of us may be in a time of winter, being pruned to produce more fruit. If only those of us in full fruit could learn not to boast of our fruitfulness, which is only by God's grace anyway, and encourage those who are experiencing a time of suffering in their lives in order to produce more fruit. If we could only understand when their suffering is through, if they have stayed successfully under the hand of God, we will benefit from the new sound that will pour from their beings. What we need to understand is that when any of us are going through a hard, desperate situation, we are in development for greater kingdom use.

We know there will be warm sun shiny days around the corner in the natural, but we don't have that same kind of trust in the spiritual. In cold weather, foliage dies so that growth can occur in the trunk of the tree, and roots can go deeper. The same happens in the spirit, but the things God can orchestrate to promote deeper growth and maturity, we rebuke. The colder the winter, the more vibrant spring will be. If you are in the midst of cold hard times right now, take heart. If your marriage looks like it is in the dead of winter, don't give up. If your financial portfolio doesn't have a "folio" to put in a "port," don't give up. Spring is coming. It may look like death all around you. Critics may have all kinds of things to say. Turn a deaf ear and keep your eyes on God and His righteousness. Surrender everything you are to Him and WORSHIP! Spring is on its way.

You won't look the same in the spring. You will be forever changed by the love of God. But the new look will look good on you. You will have become an instrument in the hand of God, made meet for the Master's use, bringing forth an original sound necessary for those in your sphere of influence to hear.

Would to God there would be more than "One" lying upon the ground, echoing surrender to the grace of God in the wake of their storm. Would to God the chorus from the tree would sing, "Holy is the Lord God Almighty Who is doing a new thing in those upon the ground. It doth not yet appear what they shall be, but when the Master is done, they shall be like Him. Then a new sound will be heard. The sound will be original, bringing redemption to the earth. Would to God when our time comes to lie upon the ground as "One," we also will have the strength to endure until through us God's breath is heard.

It is not about us, but it is about God and His glory. The cry of our heart should be "Reveal Your glory in me. I worship You." Even as Mary the mother of Jesus said, "Be it unto me according to Your word," God is looking for worshippers who will be surrendered to His will. I am sure if the truth were known, it really wasn't in Mary's plans to be the mother of Jesus. To be pregnant out of marriage in those days was a disgrace worthy of stoning. She endured criticism. Even Joseph, her finance,' was considering putting her away privately, due to the humiliation. Thank goodness he also listened to the voice of the Lord and obeyed what he was told. Sometimes our obedience and surrender to the Father's will also cost those around us. The things He wants to accomplish in the earth today through us may be embarrassing to us and to those associated with us. If it is, will we still say as Mary, "Be it unto me according to Thy word"? Am I willing to suffer embarrassment and humiliation for the cause of Christ? Had she not been willing, there would not have been a baby Jesus—at least not through Mary. Another vessel would have been chosen. God will accomplish His purpose in the earth through humanity. It might be interesting to know how many God has had to overlook to get to the "One" who is willing to be emptied of himself and used however the Father wills.

Divine Unique Ministries

More times than not, in the writings of the Old and New Testaments, those who were called out from among the rest to be instruments in the hand of God did so through much suffering, opposition, embarrassment, and criticism. If you were to look at the word of the Lord to those whose stories are highlighted throughout the scriptures with natural intellect, they never make sense. But it makes perfect sense in the Kingdom of God and acknowledges our complete dependency upon Him to bring to pass the word He has spoken in our lives. Again, if we can achieve through natural means what God has spoken within us, I doubt if it was truly a word from the Lord. We may be able to synthetically produce some sort of a replica of the vision He has put within us by natural means, but it will never contain the power of the supernatural.

> **But until each of us is taken by the Holy Spirit through His processing, our ministry will only come from our human understanding, void of the power of God.**

Ministries can be produced with accuracy in cookie cutter style from all of the bible colleges throughout the land. They contain all of the elements necessary to equip a young person to minister from the level of human understanding of the scriptures, and this is necessary for a good foundation in the Word. But until each of us is taken by the Holy Spirit through His processing, our ministry will only come from our human understanding, void of the power of God. There has to come a time when we stop being dependent upon what we know with our intellect and become dependent upon Who He *IS* in intimate relationship with the Lord Jesus Christ.

He Will Bring You Out

If you are in the midst of a crawl space I have an encouraging word for you taken from Ezekial 37. I pray you hear these words with your heart of hearts and they strengthen your inner man.

"The hand of the Lord was upon me, and He brought me out in the Spirit of the Lord and set me down in the midst of the valley;" If you are in a crawl space, know that the hand of the Lord is upon you, and He will bring you out. Be patient!

"The valley was full of bones. And He caused me to pass round about among them, and behold, there were very many (human bones) *in the open valley or plain, and behold, they were very dry. And He said unto me, Son of man, can these bones live? And I answered, O Lord God, You know!"* When you are in the midst of a crawl space and God asks you if you can live, many times our answer to the Lord is "O Lord I don't know! You know!"

"Again He said to me, Prophesy to these bones and say to them, O you dry bones, hear the word of the Lord. Thus says the Lord God to these bones: Behold, I will cause breath and spirit to enter you, and you shall live; And I will lay sinews upon you and bring up flesh upon you and cover you with skin, and I will put breath and spirit in you, and you (dry bones) *shall live; and you shall know, understand and realize that I am the Lord* (the Sovereign Ruler, Who calls forth loyalty and obedient service). *So I prophesied as I was commanded;"* Ezekial was prophesying because he was commanded. He still didn't see or feel a thing. I prophesy to you today. WORSHIP! You may not feel or see a thing but WORSHIP! You may have no emotion but WORSHIP! Worship is not based on emotion. It is an act of your will. Surrender your will to the Sovereign will of the Father, allowing Him to restore you. It may not look like worship or feel like worship. There may be no emotion or there may be uncontrollable tears. Nevertheless, declare with your mouth as an act of your will, "I WORSHIP YOU MOST HIGH GOD!" The words may come out of your spirit with such frailty the words aren't audible to anyone but God.

"And as I prophesied, there was a (thundering) *noise and behold, a shaking and trembling and a rattling, and the bones*

came together, bone to its bone. And I looked and behold, there were sinews upon (the bones) *and flesh came upon them and skin covered them over, but there was not breath or spirit in them. Then said He to me, Prophesy to the breath and spirit, son of man, and say to the breath and spirit, Thus says the Lord God; Come from the four winds, O breath and spirit, and breathe upon these slain that they may live. So I prophesied as He commanded me, and the breath and spirit came into* (the bones), *and they lived and stood up upon their feet, an exceedingly great host."*

Fill Us With Your Breath

In the midst of the darkest day of my life, after the death of my husband, I would find myself alone at home in a heap on the floor. Jerry's death following so soon after our best friend, Lee's death, seemingly knocked the breath out of me. In the midst of my floor, I would cry out not knowing what I was doing or how meaningful the words I spoke were, "Fill me with Your breath." My strength was gone but I still had children who were dependent upon me. Life must go on, but it felt like there was no breath or life in me to go on with. Fear and panic would grip me. What was I going to do? But the Spirit within me knew what to prophesy through my own mouth to raise me up as I continued to say, "Fill me with Your breath."

"Then He said to me, Son of man, these bones are the whole house of Israel. Behold, they say, Our bones are dried up and our hope is lost; and we are completely cut off." I would say unto you these bones are the body of Christ in the process of becoming the bride of Christ. In the process of becoming the mature Bride of Christ in the midst of the crawl space, it feels like all is lost, and we are cut off with no hope but God is raising us up.

"Therefore prophesy and say to them, Thus says the Lord God; Behold, I will open your graves and cause you to come up out of your graves, O My people; and I will bring you back home to the land of Israel. And you shall know that I am the Lord (your Sovereign Ruler) *when I have opened your graves and caused you*

to come up out of your graves, O My people. And I shall put My Sprit in you and you shall live and I shall place you in your own land. Then you shall know, and understand, and realize that I the Lord have spoken it and performed it, says the Lord."

The body of Christ has been in a state of widowhood. "Other Things" have crowded out our zeal for seeking first the Presence of God. We have been content for a season with the "presents" of God, but there is a cry beginning to ring out from the depths of those destined to hear the call of the Bride of Christ, "I have to have His Presence." A focus is coming in them for "One Thing"—His presence. In our seeking and surrendering to His presence, God, the Sovereign Lord, will bring us up out of our graves, out of our state of widowhood and fill us with His breath. We will stand upon our feet shod in the serene peace of God a mighty host—not a child bride. We will be a "whole bride" complete in Him, knowing with experiential understanding who He is and His righteousness.

If you are in the midst of a crawl space, and this book has been speaking directly to you keep your eyes on the Father. Understand He is developing the destiny within you. When He brings you out, the instrument you will have become will produce an original sound He will use in His continued redemption plan. If you have already experienced a crawl space, perhaps this writing has given you understanding and words to express what you know in your heart to be true. If you aren't in a crawl space, maybe you can find it in your heart to encourage someone you know who is. When they exit by the hand of God, you will be the richer for what God will produce through them that will nourish you from having known them. Regardless of who you are, I ask the Father to impart the grace in you to worship Him in the midst of everything.

17
Measuring Up In The Crawl Space

"The Lord stood upon a wall with a plumb line, with a plumb line in His hand. And the Lord said to me, 'Amos, what do you see?' And I said, 'A plumb line.' Then said the Lord, 'Behold, I am setting a plumb line as a standard in the midst of My people Israel. I will not pass by and spare them any more' (the door of mercy is shut)." (Amos 7:7,8)

A plumb line is a cord with a weight at one end called a plumb bob. It is used to determine verticality. It is directed to the center of gravity of the earth. This passage of scripture says the end of the cord is held in the Lord's hand, while gravity pulls on the plumb bob of the cord stretching the cord taunt vertically. Thus a standard of verticalness or uprightness before God is established in the midst of the people. Jesus Christ is that plumb line or standard that has been set in the midst of us.

When we gave our life to Christ, we surrendered ourselves to the Father, declaring Him to be the Lord of our lives. We immediately became caught in a bi-directional pull. We lifted our hands in surrender to God. He took our hands, and we began to walk uprightly before Him. However, the earth is still pulling at our feet. The fleshly desires and responses we used to walk in are still pulling at us to bend us back to walking in unrighteousness. The difference between the plumb line and us is choice. The plumb line remains taunt and vertically straight in the midst of the opposite pulls. We are presented with choice everyday of our lives, whether we will walk uprightly before God in the midst of opposing pulls, or surrender to the flesh becoming bent.

"Choose you this day Whom you will serve." (Joshua

24:15) Another way of saying this is, "Make your choice in your present circumstance who you will surrender to." Will you surrender to the Father and walk uprightly before Him, or will you choose the way of the world and slouch in your stance before God. He who is of the flesh will walk according to the flesh, but he who is after the spirit will walk according to the Spirit. The choice is ours.

We have taken the easy way out most of the time in our decisions or what seems to be the best for our flesh. After all, as I said earlier, it is easier to get forgiveness than permission. God's grace will forgive me even though I know I am not choosing righteousness and holiness in this current situation. It is just too hard to change and I know God understands. God understands more than we know. It is us who are void of understanding.

Love and Grace—Two Different Things

We have believed and received a grace message that frustrates the grace of God making it of no effect. We actually have made love and grace synonymous. They are not. Love covers a multitude of sins, but grace is the power to change us and redeem us out of the things that are causing us to walk bent before God. Grace is the power to change us to walk uprightly before God. Grace is God's power to grow us up into His righteousness conforming us to His will and purpose. We haven't known how to apply the grace of God in our lives to change us and take unrighteousness from us. We understand that grace saves us and takes us to heaven, but it is just as important to understand that grace changes us daily into the image of a Holy God.

It is not by our ability that we walk uprightly before God. It is by grace we walk uprightly before God. All we really are empowered to do is choose, but the pull of gravity of the world makes it hard to choose. If we could only understand the choices we make today against God's ascribed righteousness cause the grief in our lives tomorrow. When we get in the midst of the grievous situation of tomorrow, we begin to cry out for mercy or a crop failure of all the bad choices that has sown as seed in our lives.

Sometimes we receive mercy, and we know we do. We know there should have been severe consequences to the choices we made. There are other times we know we are forgiven but we still have to walk out the consequences of our choice.

The War Zone

The war is over what will rule in our lives–our flesh or the Holy Spirit of God. The word says that our faith or our personal surrender to God is what overcomes the world. As we surrender, we are to cry out "grace" to the mountain of human obstacle that is causing us to stumble and fall from the righteousness God is calling us to. He has set the standard in the midst of us. The standard is Jesus Christ. It is not a matter of Him bending to tolerate our standard. We have the mistaken idea since we cannot seem to overcome the world that is pulling at us in the weakness of our flesh, that God in His grace will overlook our slouchy stance in that area and God will bow Himself to our standard. If that is the truth, why did God send His Son to die for us? He could have overlooked and bowed to us without sending His beloved Son.

He sent His Son so that He could bring us back to the standard He has set in our midst, and He brings us back to His standard by grace through faith. We overcome by believing in and receiving the grace of God by faith in the shed blood of Jesus Christ to cleanse our lives from all unrighteousness surrendering ourselves and our rights to the Father. He will not bend to our standard. We must rise to His standard by grace through faith, leaning the entirety of our personality upon Him.

Standard is Authority

The definition of standard is the authority. The standard is the authority in any given situation. We have tried to walk in the authority of the word without walking uprightly before God and our fellow men. We want the "talk" without walking the "walk." We have hung on every word of Mark 11:23 and 24, declaring we have what we say, and we declare we have the ability to walk in that kind of authority as some have experienced. What we have failed to understand is the word "walk" in "walk in authority." We cannot "take authority" over anything or "walk in authority" until we come under authority in our personal walk of character before God adhering to His standard by grace. Those that are experiencing having what they say, aren't just talking out the word, but they are walking out the word by the grace of God in their daily lives. God help us to not just talk the talk, but walk the walk.

The words of our mouth mean nothing in the realm of the spirit as long as our integrity and character mean nothing in the realm of the earth. We have to get back to the basics. We have to habitually keep our word. We have to walk honestly in all our dealings with people. We have to stop living in the grey zone or in unrighteousness. We begin one choice at a time by grace through faith in the blood of Jesus.

In Conclusion

A new day is dawning upon the earth today. Much is being said today about us moving from a modern to a post-modern world. In the midst of physical changes there will always come spiritual changes. There is coming a new visitation of the glory of God to meet the challenges presented by a post-modern world. Historically, each new level of glory or revelation of God on the earth could not be supported by the old level of cognition supporting societal integrity. Before each new move of God things were shaken up a bit demanding a truer sense of integrity and uprightness before God and a deeper level of intimacy with God. He again is setting the plumb line in our midst preparing us for the next day of visitation.

I have heard so many say they don't understand why so many are dying or going away. They can't process the changes that are taking place. What use to work or could be counted on as stable is no longer stable. Prayer methods that use to work don't seem to be producing the same results anymore and we find our self in a dark, hard, cold crawl space. When my husband died the prayer methods that had always worked for me in the past didn't work. It seemed as though God had withdrawn His presence from me. Suddenly everything I thought I knew was confused and shaken. The methods I used to touch my Father with weren't working.

On this continuum of life I have walked a few increments past the death of my husband. What I have come to understand today has and continues to change my life. When the Father seemingly withdrew His presence from me and I found the core of my being shaken and confused with no where to turn for help to understand what was happening, I found my self with my face to the ground desperate for His presence. I know God did not take His presence from me because the Word says He will never leave us or forsake us, but I did not know this place I was in spiritually or physically. I had to seek to know my Father God in a new way.

God is not our Step-God.

We have played hide and seek with our children when they were small withdrawing our presence from them causing them to look for us. That was a fun little game; however, in real life when it feels the Father has withdrawn His presence from us in the midst of a crisis we become desperate to know Him again in a new way. I had to know my Father in a deeper more intimate way after the death of my husband. His death was contrary to anything in my belief system.

We have come to know God as a Step-God. If we do step one, step two, step three we can move the hand of God. God is not our Step-God. He wants to be known as our Father with whom we are becoming progressively and more intimately acquainted. When our steps stop working it forces us to come to know God in another way. Our tendency over time is to become more familiar with our steps and methods of knowing Him rather than *knowing Him*. When we

Before each new visitation there is a crawl space and with each visitation there is a new revelation.

155

wake up void of His presence and our methods have stopped working it makes us seek to *know Him.*

Before each new visitation there is a crawl space and with each visitation there is a new revelation. Joseph said to his brothers in Genesis 50:24, "I am going to die but God will surely visit you and bring you out of this land to the land He swore to Abraham, Isaac, and Jacob." When Joseph was alive all was well with the children of Israel in the land of Egypt. But over time the children of Israel had become slaves and in bondage to the Egyptians in a dark, hard, cold crawl space needing deliverance. God came and visited them through His servant Moses and brought them out of Egypt. Their wilderness journey was to teach them to know Him. They actually weren't very eager to learn. They told Moses to go visit with God and come back and tell them what God said. Give us step one, step two, step three and we will do it. Of course history records they didn't. God wanted an intimate relationship with them then and He wants the same thing today.

It may seem God is withdrawing His presence from us. Things may be shaking up a bit. We may find ourselves in a crawl space and our faith is no longer being sustained by His blessings. When Lee and Jerry died, Connie and I found ourselves no longer being sustained by feelings or blessings. We found ourselves desolate and desperate for His presence. When we become separated from His blessings He may be pointing out to us we have become more interested in His blessings than in knowing Him. He wants us to know Him intimately in the power of His resurrection. He wants to teach us to worship Him in the midst of the dark as well as the light and establish us in "permanent faith" unto the day of His coming without spot or wrinkle.

It is not about us anymore. It is about God and a new revelation of His glory being revealed upon the earth. God is visiting us. Even as Genesis 50:24 said, when He visits us He will bring us out. He is bringing us out of the land that we know and taking us into a new land we don't know revealing a new revelation and dimension of His glory. We live from age to age and we are in this very moment in history finding ourselves in the changing of the ages. Everything about a new visitation or revelation from God, which in essence is the dawn of new age, is unchartered. It will require a complete dependency upon His grace listening intently to His voice. The language He uses in the midst of the changing of "ages" is our circumstances. It is circumstances that speak the loudest and get our attention the most, not what we hear with our ear. Once circumstances get our attention then we are more prone to hear with our ear.

Historically when ages have changed and new revelations from God have come, we have made the mistake of disregarding the truths of the past age once the truths and revelations of the new age came forth. We rationalize since our circumstances have become unsettled and past truths don't seem to be working anymore, God must be through with that. Not true! The unsettling of circumstances is temporary to cause us to seek out the new revelation and come to a deeper and more intimate knowledge of the Lord Jesus Christ as God reveals more of Who He is. The transition is a time nothing seems to go right and the level of faith we know doesn't seem to be working. It is meant to cause us to turn our face to the wall, or in my case my face was on the floor desperately crying out for His presence. When a new revelation of faith comes it is not meant to do away with the old but build upon the old. Every age seems to think they had the ultimate revelation. In my finite understanding at this moment I think the ultimate revelation will be when our eyes are opened in that final hour to see the living temple God has been fitly joining together from the beginning of time to the end of time, from age to age. What a sight that will be to behold the unity of the faith as the revelation of all the ages comes together as one and we see the completeness of our faith throughout the ages.

In this new resurrected life Connie and I are now living since the deaths of our husbands faith has been redefined within us. We believe with even greater conviction in deliverance, healing, and prosperity but our faith is no longer the sum total of blessings that can be obtained from God. Our faith is in God

The Crawl Space

Almighty Whom we are leaning upon in the midst of *all* things. We have endured an experience where our faith was not sustained by our feelings or blessings. We didn't feel very good or very blessed to say the least when our husbands were ripped from us in their mid-forties. Inwardly everything in us died, but in the midst of that death God taught us to worship Him and in that worship our heavenly Father brought us into a depth of intimacy with Himself we never knew existed before and we know we are only scratching the surface. We are in pursuit of His presence.

I began this book in James and I want to end the same way with my paraphrased version.

> Don't think it strange when you find your self in the midst of a crawl space, circumstances you don't understand temporarily separated from outward blessings. Know this that the trial of your faith, that may seem like it will never end, is preparatory for the new glory that is about to be revealed in your life and in the life of the church. The crawl space is simply a gateway for you to become progressively and more intimately acquainted with the Lord Jesus Christ until your inward man is perfectly and fully developed with no defects. The enticing beauty of this temporal life fades in comparison to the victor's crown of life reserved for those who will remain patient in the crawl space, standing upright under temptation enduring the test of time.

Appendix
Romans Road To Righteousness

It is important what we feed into our minds and spirits while we are in a crawl space. A crawl space experience is about developing the character of God within us. It is in the crawl space we learn to walk surrendered to the Spirit of God, Christ-centered instead of surrendered to our flesh or self-centered. Paul was a man who knew how to be abased and abound. Another way of saying that is Paul knew what to do in a crawl space and how to live in the penthouse. The book of Romans is full of word that will renew our mind according to the righteousness of God through Jesus Christ developing the character of God within us. The final section of this book is a 28-day devotional based on the profound little book of Romans

As we renew our minds, the grace of God begins to transform us into His image, growing us up into Him. If our conduct of living is not changing to reflect His righteousness, maturity of character, and integrity with a deeper intimate knowledge of Who God is, I question what we are reading or the word we are hearing. If we are hearing the word but we aren't leaning into the grace of God to do what we hear or walk it out in our life, then James has something to say to us. *"But be doers of the Word* (obey the message), *and not merely listeners to it, betraying yourselves* (into deception by reasoning contrary to the Truth).*"* (James 1:22)

The book of Romans actually declares the Gospel of Christ in its entirety. The word of God has within it the power to produce life, and it will not return void. As we continually put the word into us, it will produce in us what it was originally intended to produce. The scriptures in the following pages are taken from the Amplified Bible then paraphrased to make them personal confessions over our own life as we read. It is a known fact if we read aloud the words are planted deeper into our spirit. Also, if you are serious about allowing the word of God to transform you into the image of His righteousness, ask the Holy Spirit to make the Word alive within you as you read. Use these scripture meditations over and over. These meditations from Romans could be read at least twelve times over the next year allowing the word spoken in Romans to become a part of you.

This devotional is entitled "The Romans Road To Righteousness." Righteousness is a journey by grace through faith into the redemptive blood of Jesus. I think you will agree as you practice this devotional that Paul's goal for writing Romans was to express the redemptive work of the Gospel of Christ, as well as the process of the journey down the road of righteousness. As we daily work the word into our hearts and minds, the Spirit of God can bring the life of the Word in us causing us to begin to reflect the heart of the Word. We speak confessions or affirmations over our outward man sometimes to the neglect of our inward man. These confessions are focused on our inward man to develop the character of God within us.

"When I was a child, I talked like a child, I thought like a child, I reasoned like a child; now that I have become a man, I am done with childish ways and have put them aside." (I Corinthians 13:11) We are born into the Kingdom of God as a child, but God is a God of growth. He doesn't expect us to stay as children tossed to and fro. Remember He is not coming for a child bride. He expects us to grow up into Him and His righteousness by His grace.

Prove to yourself over the next twelve months the ability and power of the word to produce the image of the righteousness of God inside of you, causing your manner of living to reflect more of who He is as you travel the Romans Road To Righteousness.

A Prayer Of Salvation—First Things First

After reading this book you may be saying, "I am certainly in a crawl space but I don't know Jesus Christ as my Savior and Lord, or I used to know Him but it has been so long since I have had anything to do with Him and I need to be re-introduced to Him." If you have never believed on the Lord Jesus Christ or received Him as your personal Lord and Savior, or if you are in a "backslidden" state, don't wait another day gambling with the eternity of your soul. You can make Him the Lord of your life right now by simply praying this prayer with me.

Dear Heavenly Father, I confess I am a sinner. I have lived my life to please my self with no regard for You. I repent of my self-centeredness. I believe You are the Son of God, the sinless sacrifice, Who loved me and gave Yourself for me dying on the cross for my sin. By the grace of God through faith in the blood of Jesus, I ask you to forgive me and deliver me from all my sin. My deliverance from sin is not by anything I can do but it is a gift from You, Father God, and I receive that gift. I declare with my mouth that Jesus Christ is the Lord of my life. I surrender all I am to the Lordship of Jesus Christ the Anointed One, leaning all of who I am upon Him.

I receive the Holy Spirit of God to live in me and be my teacher and constant companion. The Holy Spirit will instruct me in righteousness so I will live my life surrendered to the Father daily delivered from sin's dominion. I am devoted to my personal relationship with my Father God, the Lord Jesus Christ, and the Holy Spirit, and I will grow in grace and truth. I will make time to meet with You daily. One thing I desire and that is to know the depths of the love of my Father dwelling forever in His presence. I love you Father, Son, and Holy Spirit. Amen!

Father I pray for all Your children everywhere, that you would strengthen them in their inner man by Your grace. Impart the grace to worship in their hearts in the midst of any circumstance they may be facing in this very moment and in all the days to come. Let them not lose heart or become weary or faint if they are in the midst of a crawl space experience. Cause Your peace to so rule in their hearts that they become free of fear and agitating passions. Let every enemy opposed to Your righteousness come under their feet. Reveal Your Glory through them.

And now Father by Your authority I put Your name upon them.

The Lord bless you. May all you set your hand to by the direction of the Holy Spirit be blessed. May you have more than enough with which to bless others.

The Lord keep you. May He hold you safely in the palm of His hand and present you blameless at His coming.

The Lord make His face to shine upon you. May the glory of the Lord be so evidenced in your life that others are attracted to His glory.

The Lord be gracious to You. May you experience the favor, power, and ability of God to be sufficient in every event of your life.

The Lord lift up His countenance upon you. May you find that secret place in His presence that you catch His eye coming face to face in overwhelming love with the Father.

The Lord give you peace. May your heart be ruled by peace. The Lord give you peace in your home and in the lives of your children and your grandchildren. The Lord give you peace in your work place. May the enemy of your soul be overcome by the peace of God.

In the name of the Father and the Son and the Holy Spirit I put Your Name upon Your children knowing You will bless them, Amen!

God bless you as we journey together into His presence,

Sharolyn

Romans Road Of Righteousness: 28 Day Devotional

How to use this devotional

To get the maximum results from this devotional I would encourage you to read each confession aloud at least three times. As you are speaking these confessions over your life, select the one that seems to catch your attention or speak the most to your heart that day. Begin to meditate that confession. It would be good to write it down and take it with you to review throughout the day. Begin to formulate the confession into a prayer of petition to the Father. For instance, the first confession is "I am a bondservant of Jesus Christ." A prayer would be, "Father, I desire to be a bondservant to the Lord Jesus Christ. By definition bondservant means willingly living in continual obedience to the one served. I desire to live in continual obedience to You Father. Help me to live in continual obedience to You. Thank You for causing me to become a bondservant by Your grace, Your power and ability, not just in word but in everything I do, in the name of Jesus, Amen." Finally, contemplation means to be silent in His presence allowing the Holy Spirit to speak personally to you through His word. He may show you an attitude or action that needs to be corrected by His grace in your life or He may bring someone to your mind that needs encouragement. Be open to whatever He brings up in your heart and respond accordingly. God bless you as you travel The Romans Road To Righteousness.

Week One—Day One
Romans Chapter One

1. 1:1 - I am a bondservant of Jesus Christ.
2. 1:7 - I am God's beloved one called to be a saint and designated for a consecrated life: Grace and peace is mine from God my Father and from my Lord Jesus Christ.
3. 1:8 - I thank God through Jesus Christ that the report of my faith is made known to the world and is commended everywhere.
4. 1:9 - Incessantly, I always mention others when I pray.
5. 1:16 - I am not ashamed of the Gospel of Christ, for it is the power of God working unto salvation, and I believe with a personal trust and confident surrender and firm reliance.
6. 1:17 - The righteousness God ascribes is revealed in the Gospel, springing from faith, leading to faith, and arousing more faith. I am just and upright through faith and I shall live by faith.
7. 1:21 - I know and recognize Him as God, I honor and glorify Him as God and give Him thanks. I do not become futile and godless in my thinking (with vain imaginings, foolish reasoning, or stupid speculations).
8. 1:24–30 - I turn away from every kind of unrighteousness, sexual impurity, homosexuality, iniquity, covetous greed, malice, envy, jealousy, murder, strife, deceit, treachery, ill will, cruel ways, backbiting, gossip, slander, hatefulness, insolence, arrogance, boasting, inventing new forms of evil, and disobedience.
9. 1:31 - I am not without understanding, conscienceless, faithless, heartless, loveless, or merciless.

Application

Reading:

    Read each confession several times slowly. Which confession speaks the loudest in your heart today?

Meditation:

    Begin to rehearse that confession in your heart and aloud. Allow the Holy Spirit to bring the Life of the Word of that confession into your heart.

Prayer:

    Formulate that confession into a personalized prayer. Pray it back to the Father asking to be changed into the image of the Word by His grace and cause that Word to become productive in your life.

Contemplation:

    Take a few moments to be silent in His presence. Focus on Christ and His love for you. Yield yourself in true surrender to the image of His Word that is bringing life to you today. Allow the Holy Spirit to speak to you personally through that word. By grace through faith in the blood of Jesus choose the appropriate response to what is being spoken in your heart.

Week One–Day Two
Romans Chapter Two

1. 2:1 - I do not judge or condemn another, for in passing judgment on another, I condemn myself.
2. 2:4 - I do not trifle with or presume upon or despise and under estimate the wealth of God's kindness, forbearance, and longsuffering patience. I am not unmindful or ignorant of the fact that God's kindness and goodness is intended to lead me to repent (to change my mind and inner man to accept God's will).
3. 2:5 - I will not allow my heart to be calloused, stubborn, or impenitent.
4. 2:7 - By patient persistence in well doing, springing from piety, I seek glory, honor, and immortality. He will give me eternal life.
5. 2:8 - I am not self-seeking, self-centered, self-willed, or disobedient to the Truth, but I am responsive to righteousness.
6. 2:10 - Glory and honor and heart peace shall be awarded to me because I habitually do good.
7. 1:11–13 - God shows no partiality or favoritism . . . For it is not merely hearing the Law read that makes one righteous before God, but it is the doers of the Law who will be held guiltless and acquitted and justified.
8. 2:16 - God, by Jesus Christ, will judge me in regard to the things which I conceal (my hidden thoughts).

Application

Reading:

Read each confession several times slowly. Which confession speaks the loudest in your heart today?

Meditation:

Begin to rehearse that confession in your heart and aloud. Allow the Holy Spirit to bring the Life of the Word of that confession into your heart.

Prayer:

Formulate that confession into a personalized prayer. Pray it back to the Father asking to be changed into the image of the Word by His grace and cause that Word to become productive in your life.

Contemplation:

Take a few moments to be silent in His presence. Focus on Christ and His love for you. Yield yourself in true surrender to the image of His Word that is bringing life to you today. Allow the Holy Spirit to speak to you personally through that word. By grace through faith in the blood of Jesus choose the appropriate response to what is being spoken in your heart.

Week One–Day Three
Romans Chapter Two And Three

1. 2:17–24 - If I bear the name of God's Chosen and rely upon the Law and pride my self in God and my relationship to Him, and if I know and understand His will and discerningly approve the better things and have a sense of what is vital, because I have been instructed by the Law; And if I am confident that I am a guide to the blind, a light to those who are in darkness, and that I am a corrector of the foolish, a teacher of the childish, having in the Law the embodiment of knowledge and truth—Well then, if I teach others do I not teach myself? While I teach against stealing do I steal? I say not to commit adultery (but am I unchaste in action or in thought)? I abhor and loathe idols, but do I rob temples (do I appropriate for my own use what is consecrated to God, thus robbing the sanctuary and doing sacrilege? While I boast in the Law do I dishonor God by breaking the Law (stealthily infringing upon or carelessly neglecting or openly breaking it)? It is written the name of God is maligned and blasphemed among those without God because of me if I do.

2. 3:3–4 - My lack of faith and my faithlessness does not nullify or make ineffective, or void the faithfulness of God and His fidelity to His word. Let God be found true though every human being is false and a liar that God may be justified and shown to be upright in what He says, and prevail when He is judged by sinful men.

3. 3:9–10 - All men are under sin as it is written, none is righteous, just, truthful, upright, and conscientious, no, not one.

4. 3:17–18 - I have experience with the way of peace. I recognize the peaceful way and the reverential fear of God is before my eyes.

Application

Reading:

Read each confession several times slowly. Which confession speaks the loudest in your heart today?

Meditation:

Begin to rehearse that confession in your heart and aloud. Allow the Holy Spirit to bring the Life of the Word of that confession into your heart.

Prayer:

Formulate that confession into a personalized prayer. Pray it back to the Father asking to be changed into the image of the Word by His grace and cause that Word to become productive in your life.

Contemplation:

Take a few moments to be silent in His presence. Focus on Christ and His love for you. Yield yourself in true surrender to the image of His Word that is bringing life to you today. Allow the Holy Spirit to speak to you personally through that word. By grace through faith in the blood of Jesus choose the appropriate response to what is being spoken in your heart.

Week One–Day Four
Romans Chapter Three

1. 3:20 - I will not be justified in His sight by observing the works prescribed by the Law. The real function of the Law is to make me recognize and be conscious of sin (not mere perception, but an acquaintance with sin which works toward repentance, faith, and holy character).
2. 3:21 - The righteousness of God has been revealed independently and altogether apart from the Law, although actually it is confirmed by the Law and the Prophets.
3. 3:22 - The righteousness of God comes to me by believing with personal trust and confident reliance on Jesus Christ (the Messiah)
4. 3:23 - I have sinned and have fallen short of the honor and glory, which God bestows and receives.
5. 3:24–26 - I am justified and made upright and in right standing with God, freely and gratuitously by His grace in Christ Jesus whom God put forward as a mercy seat and propitiation by His blood (the cleansing and life-giving sacrifice of atonement and reconciliation, to be received through faith. This was to show God's righteousness, because in His divine forbearance He had passed over and ignored my former sins without punishment. God demonstrated and proved at the present time that He Himself is righteous and that He justifies and accepts me as righteous because of true faith in Jesus.
6. 3:27–28 -My pride and boasting are excluded on the principle of faith for I hold that I am justified and made upright by faith independent of and distinctly apart from good deeds. (The observance of the Law has nothing to do with justification.)
7. 3:31 - Do I then by faith make the Law of no effect, overthrow it, or make it a dead letter? Certainly not! On the contrary, I confirm and establish and uphold the Law.

Application

Reading:

Read each confession several times slowly. Which confession speaks the loudest in your heart today?

Meditation:

Begin to rehearse that confession in your heart and aloud. Allow the Holy Spirit to bring the Life of the Word of that confession into your heart.

Prayer:

Formulate that confession into a personalized prayer. Pray it back to the Father asking to be changed into the image of the Word by His grace and cause that Word to become productive in your life.

Contemplation:

Take a few moments to be silent in His presence. Focus on Christ and His love for you. Yield yourself in true surrender to the image of His Word that is bringing life to you today. Allow the Holy Spirit to speak to you personally through that word. By grace through faith in the blood of Jesus choose the appropriate response to what is being spoken in your heart.

Week One–Day Five
Roman Chapter Four

1. 4:3 -Abraham believed in (trusted in) God, and it was credited to his account as righteousness (right living and right standing with God).
2. 4:6 - David congratulates the man and pronounces a blessing on him to whom God credits righteousness apart from the works he does.
3. 4:7–8 - I am blessed happy and to be envied because my iniquities are forgiven and my sins are covered up and completely buried, and because the Lord takes no account of my sin and does not reckon it against me.
4. 4:13–16 - The promise to Abraham and his posterity of inheriting the world, did not come through (observing the commands of) the Law, but through the righteousness of faith. Therefore, my inheriting the promise is the outcome of faith and depends entirely on faith, in order that it might be given as an act of grace.
5. 4:17 - God gives life to the dead and speaks of the non-existent things that (He has foretold and promised as if they [already] existed.)
6. 4:20 - No unbelief or distrust will make me waver (doubtingly question) concerning the promise of God, but I will grow strong and be empowered by faith as I give praise and glory to God.
7. 4:21 - I am fully satisfied and assured that God is able and mighty to keep His word and do what He has promised for me.
8. 4:24–25 - (Righteousness, standing acceptable to God) will be granted and credited to me also because I believe in (trust in, adhere to, and rely on) God, Who raised Jesus my Lord from the dead, Who was betrayed and put to death because of my misdeeds and was raised to secure my justification (my acquittal), making my account balance and absolving me from all guilt before God.

Application

Reading:

Read each confession several times slowly. Which confession speaks the loudest in your heart today?

Meditation:

Begin to rehearse that confession in your heart and aloud. Allow the Holy Spirit to bring the Life of the Word of that confession into your heart.

Prayer:

Formulate that confession into a personalized prayer. Pray it back to the Father asking to be changed into the image of the Word by His grace and cause that Word to become productive in your life.

Contemplation:

Take a few moments to be silent in His presence. Focus on Christ and His love for you. Yield yourself in true surrender to the image of His Word that is bringing life to you today. Allow the Holy Spirit to speak to you personally through that word. By grace through faith in the blood of Jesus choose the appropriate response to what is being spoken in your heart.

Week One–Day Six
Romans Chapter Five

1. 5:1 - Since I am justified with God through faith, I have the peace of reconciliation to hold and to enjoy, peace with God through my Lord Jesus Christ (the Messiah, the Anointed One).
2. 5:2 - Through Jesus Christ, I have access by faith into the grace of God in which I firmly and safely stand. And I will rejoice and exult in my hope of experiencing and enjoying the glory of God.
3. 5:3–5 - I will be full of joy now and exult and triumph in my troubles and rejoice in my sufferings knowing that pressure and affliction and hardship produce patient and unswerving endurance. Endurance develops maturity of character (approved faith and tried integrity). And character of this sort produces the habit of joyful and confident hope of eternal salvation. Such hope never disappoints or deludes or shames me, for God's love has been poured out in my heart through the Holy Spirit who has been given to me.
4. 5:6–8 - While I was yet in weakness (powerless to help myself) at the fitting time Christ died for me. God shows and clearly proves His own love for me by the fact that while I was still a sinner, Christ died for me.
5. 5:9–10 - Since I am justified by Christ's blood, how much more certain is it that I shall be saved by Him from the indignation and wrath of God, for if while I was an enemy I was reconciled to God through the death of His Son, it is much more certain, now that I am reconciled, that I shall be saved (daily delivered from sin's dominion) through His resurrection life.

Application

Reading:

Read each confession several times slowly. Which confession speaks the loudest in your heart today?

Meditation:

Begin to rehearse that confession in your heart and aloud. Allow the Holy Spirit to bring the Life of the Word of that confession into your heart.

Prayer:

Formulate that confession into a personalized prayer. Pray it back to the Father asking to be changed into the image of the Word by His grace and cause that Word to become productive in your life.

Contemplation:

Take a few moments to be silent in His presence. Focus on Christ and His love for you. Yield yourself in true surrender to the image of His Word that is bringing life to you today. Allow the Holy Spirit to speak to you personally through that word. By grace through faith in the blood of Jesus choose the appropriate response to what is being spoken in your heart.

Week One–Day Seven
Romans Chapter Five

1. 5:11 - I rejoice and exultingly glory in God in His love and perfection through my Lord Jesus Christ through whom I have now received and enjoy my reconciliation.
2. 5:12–15 - Sin came into the world through one man, and death as a result of sin came to all men because all men sinned. To be sure sin was in the world before ever the Law was given, but sin is not charged to men's account where there is no law to transgress. Yet death held sway from Adam to Moses (the lawgiver), even over those who did not transgress as Adam did. But God's free gift is not at all to be compared to the trespass (His grace is out of proportion to the fall of man). For if many died through one man's falling away, much more profusely did God's grace and the free gift that comes through the undeserved favor of the one Man Jesus Christ abound and overflow to and for the benefit of many.
3. 5:17 - If because of one man's trespass (laps, offense) death reigned through that one, much more surely will those who receive God's overflowing grace and the free gift of righteousness reign as kings in life through the one Man Jesus Christ (the Messiah, the Anointed One). I have received God's overflowing grace and the free gift of righteousness. I reign as a king in life through the one Man Jesus Christ (the Messiah the Anointed One).
4. 5:19 - I am not disobedient, failing to hear, heedless, or careless leading others astray.
5. 5:20–21 - Where sin increased and abounded, grace has surpassed it and increased the more and super abounded, so that as sin has reigned in death, grace might reign also through righteousness which issues in eternal life through Jesus Christ our Lord.

Application

Reading:

Read each confession several times slowly. Which confession speaks the loudest in your heart today?

Meditation:

Begin to rehearse that confession in your heart and aloud. Allow the Holy Spirit to bring the Life of the Word of that confession into your heart.

Prayer:

Formulate that confession into a personalized prayer. Pray it back to the Father asking to be changed into the image of the Word by His grace and cause that Word to become productive in your life.

Contemplation:

Take a few moments to be silent in His presence. Focus on Christ and His love for you. Yield yourself in true surrender to the image of His Word that is bringing life to you today. Allow the Holy Spirit to speak to you personally through that word. By grace through faith in the blood of Jesus choose the appropriate response to what is being spoken in your heart.

Week Two–Day One
Romans Chapter Six

1. 6:1–2 - What shall I say to all this? Should I remain in sin in order that God's grace may multiply and overflow? Certainly not! I have died to sin therefore I cannot live in it any longer.
2. 6:3 - I am not ignorant of the fact that when I was baptized into Christ I was baptized into His death.
3. 6:4 - I have been buried with Christ by the baptism into death, so that just as Christ was raised from the dead by the glorious power of the Father, so I too might habitually live and behave in newness of life.
4. 6:5 - I have become one with Christ by sharing a death like His, so shall I also be one with Him in sharing His resurrection by a new life lived for God.
5. 6:6–7 - My old unrenewed self (self-centeredness) was nailed to the cross with Him in order that my body of sin might be made ineffective and inactive for evil, that I might no longer be a slave of sin. For when a man dies, he is freed from the power of sin among men.
6. 6:8 - I have died with Christ, therefore I shall also live with Him.
7. 6:10–11 - Even as Christ died to sin ending His relation to it and the life that He lives He is living to God in unbroken fellowship with Him. Even so I consider myself also dead to sin and my relation to it broken, but alive to God living in unbroken fellowship with Him in Christ Jesus.
8. 6:12 - I will not let sin rule as king in my mortal body to make me yield to its cravings and be subject to its lusts and evil passions.
9. 6:13 - I offer and yield myself to God as though I have been raised from the dead to perpetual life, and my bodily members and faculties to God, presenting them as implements of righteousness.

Application

Reading:

Read each confession several times slowly. Which confession speaks the loudest in your heart today?

Meditation:

Begin to rehearse that confession in your heart and aloud. Allow the Holy Spirit to bring the Life of the Word of that confession into your heart.

Prayer:

Formulate that confession into a personalized prayer. Pray it back to the Father asking to be changed into the image of the Word by His grace and cause that Word to become productive in your life.

Contemplation:

Take a few moments to be silent in His presence. Focus on Christ and His love for you. Yield yourself in true surrender to the image of His Word that is bringing life to you today. Allow the Holy Spirit to speak to you personally through that word. By grace through faith in the blood of Jesus choose the appropriate response to what is being spoken in your heart.

Week Two–Day Two
Romans Chapter Six

1. 6:14–15 - Sin shall not exert dominion over me since I am not under Law but under Grace. What then should I conclude? Shall I sin because I live not under the Law but under God's favor and mercy? Certainly not!
2. 6:16 - If I continually surrender myself to anyone to do his will, I am a slave of him whom I obey, whether that be to sin, which leads to death, or to obedience which leads to righteousness (right doing and right standing with God).
3. 6:17 - I once was a slave to sin, but now I have become obedient with all my heart to the standard of teaching in which I was instructed and to which I was committed.
4. 6:18 - I have been set free from sin and have become the servant of righteousness (of conformity to the divine will in thought, purpose, and action).
5. 6:19 - As I yielded my bodily members (and faculties) as servants to impurity and ever increasing lawlessness, so now I yield my bodily member (and faculties) once for all as servants to righteousness (right being and doing) (which leads) to sanctification.
6. 6:20 - When I was a slave to sin I was free in regard to righteousness. But then what benefit (return) did I get from the things of which I am now ashamed? (None) for the end of those things is death.
7. 6:22 - But now since I have been set free from sin and have become a slave of God, I have my present reward in holiness and its end is eternal life.
8. 6:23 - The wages that sin pays is death, but the (bountiful) free gift of God is eternal life through Jesus Christ our Lord.

Application

Reading:

Read each confession several times slowly. Which confession speaks the loudest in your heart today?

Meditation:

Begin to rehearse that confession in your heart and aloud. Allow the Holy Spirit to bring the Life of the Word of that confession into your heart.

Prayer:

Formulate that confession into a personalized prayer. Pray it back to the Father asking to be changed into the image of the Word by His grace and cause that Word to become productive in your life.

Contemplation:

Take a few moments to be silent in His presence. Focus on Christ and His love for you. Yield yourself in true surrender to the image of His Word that is bringing life to you today. Allow the Holy Spirit to speak to you personally through that word. By grace through faith in the blood of Jesus choose the appropriate response to what is being spoken in your heart.

Week Two–Day Three
Romans Chapter Seven

1. 7:1–4 - Legal claims have power over a person only for as long as he is alive. For instance, a married woman is bound by law to her husband as long as he lives; but if her husband dies, she is loosed and discharged from the law concerning her husband. Accordingly, she will be held an adulteress if she unites herself to another man while her husband lives. But if her husband dies, the marriage law no longer is binding on her (she is free from the law); and if she unites herself to another man, she is not an adulteress. Likewise, I have undergone death as to the Law through the crucified body of Christ, so that now I may belong to Another, to Him who was raised from the dead in order that I may bear fruit for God.

2. 7:5–6 - When I was living in the flesh (a mere physical life), the sinful passions that were awakened and aroused up by what the Law makes sin were constantly operating in my natural powers (in my bodily organs, in the sensitive appetites and wills of the flesh), so that I bore fruit for death. Now, I am discharged from the Law, having died to what once restrained and held me captive. So now I serve not under obedience to the old code of written regulations but under obedience to the prompting of the Spirit in newness of life.

3. 7:7 - The Law is not identical with sin. Nevertheless, if it had not been for the Law, I would not have recognized sin or have known its meaning. (For instance) I would not have known about covetousness (would have had no consciousness of sin or sense of guilt) if the Law had not (repeatedly) said, "You shall not covet and have an evil desire," (for one thing and another).

4. 7:8—But sin finding opportunity in the commandment to express itself got a hold on me and aroused and stimulated all kinds of forbidden desires (lust, covetousness). For without the Law sin is dead (the sense of it is inactive and a lifeless thing).

Application

Reading:
Read each confession several times slowly. Which confession speaks the loudest in your heart today?

Meditation:
Begin to rehearse that confession in your heart and aloud. Allow the Holy Spirit to bring the Life of the Word of that confession into your heart.

Prayer:
Formulate that confession into a personalized prayer. Pray it back to the Father asking to be changed into the image of the Word by His grace and cause that Word to become productive in your life.

Contemplation:
Take a few moments to be silent in His presence. Focus on Christ and His love for you. Yield yourself in true surrender to the image of His Word that is bringing life to you today. Allow the Holy Spirit to speak to you personally through that word. By grace through faith in the blood of Jesus choose the appropriate response to what is being spoken in your heart.

Week Two–Day Four
Romans Chapter Seven

1. 7:9–11 - Once I was alive, but quite apart from and unconscious of the Law. But when the commandment came, sin lived again and I died. And the very legal ordinance, which was designed and intended to bring life, actually proved to mean to me death. Sin, seizing the opportunity and getting a hold on me by taking its incentive from the commandment, beguiled me and entrapped and cheated me, and using the Law as a weapon killed me.

2. 7:12–13 - The Law therefore is holy, and each commandment is holy and just and good. Did that which is good then prove fatal (bringing death) to me? Certainly Not! It was sin working death in me by using this good thing (as a weapon), in order that through the commandment sin might be shown up clearly to be sin, that the extreme malignity and immeasurable sinfulness of sin might plainly appear.

3. 7:14–15 - I know that the Law is spiritual; but I am a creature of the flesh (carnal and unspiritual), having been sold into slavery under the control of sin. For I do not understand my own actions (I am baffled and bewildered). I do not practice or accomplish what I wish, but I do the very thing that I loathe (which my moral instinct condemns).

4. 7:18 - I know that nothing good dwells within me that is in my flesh. I can will what is right, but I cannot perform it. I have the intention and urge to do what is right, but no power to carry it out.

5. 7:21–23 - I find it to be a law (rule of action of my being) that when I want to do what is right and good, evil is ever present with me, and I am subject to its insistent demands. I endorse and delight in the Law of God in my inmost self with my new nature, but I discern in my bodily members—in the sensitive appetites and wills of the flesh—a different law as war against the law of my mind (my rea-

son) and making me a prisoner to the law of sin that dwells in my bodily organs (in the sensitive appetites and wills of the flesh).
6. 7:24–25 - O unhappy and pitiable and wretched man that I am! Who will release and deliver me from (the shackles of) this body of death? I thank God that He will deliver me through Jesus Christ the Anointed One our Lord! So then indeed I of myself with the mind and heart, serve the Law of God, but with the flesh, the law of sin.

Application

Reading:

Read each confession several times slowly. Which confession speaks the loudest in your heart today?

Meditation:

Begin to rehearse that confession in your heart and aloud. Allow the Holy Spirit to bring the Life of the Word of that confession into your heart.

Prayer:

Formulate that confession into a personalized prayer. Pray it back to the Father asking to be changed into the image of the Word by His grace and cause that Word to become productive in your life.

Contemplation:

Take a few moments to be silent in His presence. Focus on Christ and His love for you. Yield yourself in true surrender to the image of His Word that is bringing life to you today. Allow the Holy Spirit to speak to you personally through that word. By grace through faith in the blood of Jesus choose the appropriate response to what is being spoken in your heart.

Week Two–Day Five
Romans Chapter Eight

1. 8:1 - Therefore there is now no condemnation (no adjudging guilty of wrong) for me because I am in Christ Jesus. I live and walk not after the dictates of the flesh, but after the dictates of the Spirit.
2. 8:2 - The law of the Spirit of life, which is in Christ Jesus (the law of our new being), has freed me from the law of sin and of death.
3. 8:3 - For God has done what the Law of God could not do, (its power) being weakened by my flesh (the entire nature of man without the Holy Spirit). Sending His own Son in the guise of sinful flesh and as an offering for sin, God condemned sin in the flesh subdued, overcame, deprived it of its power over me because I accept that sacrifice.
4. 8:4 - The righteous and just requirements of the Law might be fully met in me because I live and move not in the ways of the flesh, but in the ways of the Spirit. My life is not governed by the standards and according to the dictates of the flesh, but controlled by the Holy Spirit.
5. 8:5 - I am not as one who lives according to the flesh and controlled by its unholy desires, nor do I set my mind on and pursue those things which gratify the flesh, but I live according to the Spirit, and I am controlled by the desires of the Spirit, setting my mind on and seeking those things which gratify the Holy Spirit.
6. 8:6 - I do not live after the mind of the flesh (which is sense and reason without the Holy Spirit, which is death. But I live according to the mind of the Holy Spirit, which is life and soul peace, both now and forever.

Application

Reading:

Read each confession several times slowly. Which confession speaks the loudest in your heart today?

Meditation:

Begin to rehearse that confession in your heart and aloud. Allow the Holy Spirit to bring the Life of the Word of that confession into your heart.

Prayer:

Formulate that confession into a personalized prayer. Pray it back to the Father asking to be changed into the image of the Word by His grace and cause that Word to become productive in your life.

Contemplation:

Take a few moments to be silent in His presence. Focus on Christ and His love for you. Yield yourself in true surrender to the image of His Word that is bringing life to you today. Allow the Holy Spirit to speak to you personally through that word. By grace through faith in the blood of Jesus choose the appropriate response to what is being spoken in your heart.

WEEK TWO–Day Six
Roman Chapter Eight

1. 8:7 - I do not live after the mind of the flesh with its carnal thoughts and purposes. It is hostile to God, for it does not submit itself to God's Law; indeed it cannot.
2. 8:8 - I am not living the life of the flesh—catering to the appetites and impulses of my carnal nature—because I desire to please and satisfy God and be acceptable to Him.
3. 8:9 - I am not living a life of the flesh, but I am living a life of the Spirit because the Holy Spirit really dwells in me directing and controlling me.
4. 8:10 - Christ lives in me so even though my natural body is dead because of sin and guilt, my spirit is alive because of the righteousness that He imputes to me.
5. 8:11 - The Spirit of God who raised Jesus from the dead dwells in me, so He who raised up Christ Jesus from the dead will also restore to life my mortal, short-lived, perishable body through His Spirit Who dwells in me.
6. 8:12 - I am a debtor, but not to the flesh (I am not obligated to my carnal nature), to live (a life ruled by the standards set up by the dictates) of my flesh.
7. 8:13 - If I live according to (the dictates of) the flesh, I will surely die, but if through the power of the Holy Spirit, I am habitually putting to death (making extinct, deadening) the evil deeds prompted by my body, so I will (really and genuinely) live forever.
8. 8:14 - I am led by the Spirit of God, therefore, I am a child of God.
9. 8:15 - I am no longer under bondage to fear, but I have received the Spirit of adoption (the Sprit producing sonship) in the bliss of which I cry Abba! Father!

Application

Reading:
Read each confession several times slowly. Which confession speaks the loudest in your heart today?

Meditation:
Begin to rehearse that confession in your heart and aloud. Allow the Holy Spirit to bring the Life of the Word of that confession into your heart.

Prayer:
Formulate that confession into a personalized prayer. Pray it back to the Father asking to be changed into the image of the Word by His grace and cause that Word to become productive in your life.

Contemplation:
Take a few moments to be silent in His presence. Focus on Christ and His love for you. Yield yourself in true surrender to the image of His Word that is bringing life to you today. Allow the Holy Spirit to speak to you personally through that word. By grace through faith in the blood of Jesus choose the appropriate response to what is being spoken in your heart.

Week Two–Day Seven
Romans Chapter Eight

1. 8:16,18 - The Spirit Himself testifies together with my own spirit assuring me that I am a child of God, therefore, I am an heir of God and a joint heir with Christ (sharing His inheritance with Him), only I must share His suffering if I am to share His glory. But so what if I do? I consider that the sufferings of this present time are not worth being compared with the glory that is about to be revealed to me and in me and for me and conferred on me.

2. 8:19–25 - All creation waits expectantly and longs earnestly for God's children to be made known. Nature itself will be set free from its bondage to decay and corruption into the glorious freedom of God's children. We know that the whole creation of irrational creatures have been moaning together in the pains of labor until now. And not only the creation, but I too, who have and enjoy the first fruits of the Holy Spirit, a foretaste of the blissful things to come, groan inwardly as I wait for the redemption of my body (from sensuality and the grave, which will reveal) and my adoption (my manifestation as God's son). For in this hope I was saved. But hope (the object of), which is seen, is not hope. For how can I hope for what I already see? But if I hope for what is still unseen by me, I wait for it with patience and composure.

3. 8:26–27 - The Holy Spirit comes to my aid and bears me up in my weakness; for I do not know what prayer to offer nor how to offer it worthily as I ought, but the Spirit Himself goes to meet my supplications and pleads in my behalf with unspeakable yearnings and groanings too deep for utterance. And He Who searches the hearts of men, knows what is in the mind of the Holy Spirit (what His intent is) because the Spirit intercedes and pleads before God in behalf of the saints, according to and in harmony with God's will.

Application

Reading:
Read each confession several times slowly. Which confession speaks the loudest in your heart today?

Meditation:
Begin to rehearse that confession in your heart and aloud. Allow the Holy Spirit to bring the Life of the Word of that confession into your heart.

Prayer:
Formulate that confession into a personalized prayer. Pray it back to the Father asking to be changed into the image of the Word by His grace and cause that Word to become productive in your life.

Contemplation:
Take a few moments to be silent in His presence. Focus on Christ and His love for you. Yield yourself in true surrender to the image of His Word that is bringing life to you today. Allow the Holy Spirit to speak to you personally through that word. By grace through faith in the blood of Jesus choose the appropriate response to what is being spoken in your heart.

Week Three–Day One
Romans Chapter Eight

1. 8:28 - I am assured and know that (God being partner in my labor) all things are working together and are (fitting into a plan) for good to and for me because I love God, and I am called according to His design and purpose.
2. 8:29 - He foreknew me and destined me from the beginning to be molded into the image of His Son (and share inwardly His likeness), that He might become the firstborn among many brethren.
3. 8:30 - He has foreordained me, called me, justified me (acquitted, made righteous, putting me into right standing with Himself) and glorified me (raising me to a heavenly dignity and condition or state of being).
4. 8:31 - God is for me, so who can be against me? (Who can be my foe since God in on my side?)
5. 8:32 - He who did not withhold or spare (even) His own Son but gave Him up for us all, will He not also with Him freely and graciously give me all (other) things?
6. 8:33–35 - Who shall bring any charge against God's elect (when it is) God Who justifies. Who shall accuse or impeach those whom God has chosen? Will God, who acquits me? Who is there to condemn me? Will Christ Jesus (the Messiah), Who died, or rather Who was raised from the dead, Who is at the right hand of God actually pleading as He intercedes for me? Who shall ever separate me from Christ's love? Shall suffering and affliction and tribulation? Or calamity and distress? Or persecution or hunger or destitution or peril or sword?
7. 8:36–37 - For Thy sake, we are put to death all the day long as we are regarded and counted as a sheep for the slaughter. Yet amid all these things, I am more than a conqueror, and I gain a surpassing victory through Him Who loved me.

8. 8:38–39 - I am persuaded beyond doubt that neither death nor life, nor angels nor principalities, nor things impending and threatening, nor things to come, nor powers nor height, nor depth, nor any thing else in all creation will be able to separate me from the love of God, which is in Christ Jesus my Lord.

Application

Reading:
Read each confession several times slowly. Which confession speaks the loudest in your heart today?

Meditation:
Begin to rehearse that confession in your heart and aloud. Allow the Holy Spirit to bring the Life of the Word of that confession into your heart.

Prayer:
Formulate that confession into a personalized prayer. Pray it back to the Father asking to be changed into the image of the Word by His grace and cause that Word to become productive in your life.

Contemplation:
Take a few moments to be silent in His presence. Focus on Christ and His love for you. Yield yourself in true surrender to the image of His Word that is bringing life to you today. Allow the Holy Spirit to speak to you personally through that word. By grace through faith in the blood of Jesus choose the appropriate response to what is being spoken in your heart.

Week Three–Day Two
Romans Chapter Nine (The Sovereignty of God)

1. 9:8 - It is not the children of the body (of Abraham) who are made God's children, but it is the offspring to whom the promise applies that shall be counted (as Abraham's true) descendants. For this is what the promise said, "About this time (next year) will I return, and Sarah shall have a son." And not only that, but this too, Rebecca conceived (two sons under exactly the same circumstances) by our forefather Isaac, and the children were yet unborn and had so far done nothing either good or evil. Even so, in order further to carry out God's purpose of selection (election, choice), which depends not on works or what men can do, but on Him Who calls (them). It was said to her that the elder (son) would serve the younger (son). As it is written, "Jacob have I loved, but Esau have I hated" (held in relative disregard in comparison with My feeling for Jacob). What shall we conclude then? Is there injustice upon God's part? Certainly not! For He says to Moses, "I will have mercy on whom I will have mercy, and I will have compassion (pity) on whom I will have compassion."

2. 9:16 - So then God's gift is not a question of human will and human effort, but of God's mercy, (It depends not on my own willingness, nor on my strenuous exertion as in running a race, but on God's having mercy on me).

3. 9:17–19 - The Scripture says to Pharaoh, "I have raised you up for this very purpose of displaying My power in (dealing with) you, so that My name may be proclaimed the whole world over." So then He has mercy on whomever He wills (chooses) and He hardens (makes stubborn and unyielding the heart of) whomever He wills. You will say to me, "Why then does He still find fault and blame us (for sinning)? For who can resist and withstand His will?"

4. 9:20–21 - Who am I a mere man, to criticize and contradict and answer back to God? Will what is formed say to him that formed it, "Why have you made me thus?" Has the potter no right over the clay, to make out of the same mass (lump) one vessel for beauty and distinction and honorable use, and another for menial or ignoble and dishonorable use.

Application

Reading:
Read each confession several times slowly. Which confession speaks the loudest in your heart today?

Meditation:
Begin to rehearse that confession in your heart and aloud. Allow the Holy Spirit to bring the Life of the Word of that confession into your heart.

Prayer:
Formulate that confession into a personalized prayer. Pray it back to the Father asking to be changed into the image of the Word by His grace and cause that Word to become productive in your life.

Contemplation:
Take a few moments to be silent in His presence. Focus on Christ and His love for you. Yield yourself in true surrender to the image of His Word that is bringing life to you today. Allow the Holy Spirit to speak to you personally through that word. By grace through faith in the blood of Jesus choose the appropriate response to what is being spoken in your heart.

Week Three–Day Three
Romans Chapter Nine

1. 9:22–24 - What if God, although fully intending to show (the awfulness of) His wrath and to make known His power and authority, has tolerated with much patience the vessels (objects) of (His) anger which are ripe for destruction? And (what if) He thus purposes to make known and show the wealth of His glory in (dealing with) the vessels (objects) of His mercy, which He has prepared beforehand for glory, even including ourselves whom He has called, not only from among the Jews (God's chosen), but also from among the Gentiles (heathen)?

2. 9:27–28 - Though the number of the sons of Israel be like the sand of the sea, only the remnant (a small part of them) will be saved from perdition, condemnation, judgment! For the Lord will execute His sentence upon the earth (He will conclude and close His account with men completely and without delay), rigorously cutting it short in His justice.

3. 9:30–31 - Sinners who did not follow after righteousness (who did not seek salvation by right relationship to God) have attained it by faith (a righteousness imputed by God, based on and produced by faith), whereas Israel, though ever in pursuit of the law (for the securing) of righteousness (right standing with God), actually did not succeed in fulfilling the Law. For what reason? Because they pursued it not through faith, but by relying (instead) on the merit of their works (they did not depend on faith but on what they could do). They have stumbled over the Stumbling Stone. I pursue righteousness (right standing with God) by faith. I do not rely on the merit of my works. I depend on faith, not on what I can do. Therefore, I will not stumble over the Stumbling Stone.

4. 9:33 - I believe in the Rock, the Stone laid in Zion. I adhere to, trust in, and rely on Him, and I shall not be put to shame, nor be disappointed in my expectations.

Application

Reading:

Read each confession several times slowly. Which confession speaks the loudest in your heart today?

Meditation:

Begin to rehearse that confession in your heart and aloud. Allow the Holy Spirit to bring the Life of the Word of that confession into your heart.

Prayer:

Formulate that confession into a personalized prayer. Pray it back to the Father asking to be changed into the image of the Word by His grace and cause that Word to become productive in your life.

Contemplation:

Take a few moments to be silent in His presence. Focus on Christ and His love for you. Yield yourself in true surrender to the image of His Word that is bringing life to you today. Allow the Holy Spirit to speak to you personally through that word. By grace through faith in the blood of Jesus choose the appropriate response to what is being spoken in your heart.

Week Three–Day Four
Romans Chapter Ten

1. 10:1 - With all my heart's desire and goodwill for the nations, I long and pray to God that they may be saved.
2. 10:2 - I have zeal and enthusiasm for God, and it is enlightened according to correct and vital knowledge.
3. 10:3 - I am not ignorant of the righteousness God ascribes, which makes me acceptable to Him in word, thought, and deed, and I am not seeking to establish a righteousness (a means of salvation) of my own. I obey and submit myself to God's righteousness.
4. 10:4 - The purpose of the Law is fulfilled in Christ as the means of righteousness (right relationship to God) for everyone who trusts in, and adheres to, and relies on Him.
5. 10:8–9 - The Word (God's message in Christ) is on my lips and in my heart; that is the Word, the message, the basis and object of faith, which we preach. Because if I confess with my lips that Jesus is Lord and in my heart believe (adhere to, trust in, and rely on the truth) that God raised Jesus from the dead, I will be saved.
6. 10:10 - With my heart I believe (adhere to, trust in, and rely on Christ) and so I am justified (declared righteous and acceptable to God), and with my mouth I confess (declare openly and speak out freely) my faith and confirm my salvation.
7. 10:11 - The Scripture says, "No one who believes in Christ (who adheres to, relies on, and trusts in Christ) will ever be put to shame or be disappointed." I believe in Christ.
8. 10:13 - EVERYONE, who calls upon the name of the Lord (invoking Him as Lord will be saved.

Application

Reading:

Read each confession several times slowly. Which confession speaks the loudest in your heart today?

Meditation:

Begin to rehearse that confession in your heart and aloud. Allow the Holy Spirit to bring the Life of the Word of that confession into your heart.

Prayer:

Formulate that confession into a personalized prayer. Pray it back to the Father asking to be changed into the image of the Word by His grace and cause that Word to become productive in your life.

Contemplation:

Take a few moments to be silent in His presence. Focus on Christ and His love for you. Yield yourself in true surrender to the image of His Word that is bringing life to you today. Allow the Holy Spirit to speak to you personally through that word. By grace through faith in the blood of Jesus choose the appropriate response to what is being spoken in your heart.

Week Three–Day Five
Romans Chapter Ten

1. 10:14–15 - How are people to call upon Christ, Whom they have not believed in, in Whom they have no faith, on Whom they have no reliance? And how are they to believe in Him (adhere to, trust in, and rely upon Him) of Whom they have never heard? And how are they to hear without a preacher? And how shall the preachers go unless they sent?
2. 10:17 - Faith comes by hearing what is told, and what is heard comes by the preaching of the message that came from the lips of Christ the Messiah Himself.
3. 10:18 - But I ask, "Have they not heard?" Indeed they have; for the Scripture says, "Their voice (that of nature bearing God's message) has gone out to all the earth, and their words to the far bounds of the world."
4. 10:20–21 - "I have been found by those who did not seek Me; I have shown (revealed) Myself to those who did not (consciously) ask for Me." But of Israel he says, "All day long I have stretched out My hands to a people unyielding and disobedient and self-willed to a faultfinding, contrary, and contradicting people." (Father, I desire not to be unyielding, disobedient, self-willed, faultfinding, contrary, or contradictory.)

Application

Reading:

Read each confession several times slowly. Which confession speaks the loudest in your heart today?

Meditation:

Begin to rehearse that confession in your heart and aloud. Allow the Holy Spirit to bring the Life of the Word of that confession into your heart.

Prayer:

Formulate that confession into a personalized prayer. Pray it back to the Father asking to be changed into the image of the Word by His grace and cause that Word to become productive in your life.

Contemplation:

Take a few moments to be silent in His presence. Focus on Christ and His love for you. Yield yourself in true surrender to the image of His Word that is bringing life to you today. Allow the Holy Spirit to speak to you personally through that word. By grace through faith in the blood of Jesus choose the appropriate response to what is being spoken in your heart.

Week Three–Day Six
Romans Chapter Eleven

1. 11:1, 5–6 - Has God totally rejected and disowned His people? Of course not! God's people have a destiny He has marked out and appointed and foreknown from the beginning. God has kept for Himself, a remnant, who have not bowed their knee to idols. At this present time, there is a remnant (a small believing minority), selected (chosen) by grace (by God's unmerited favor and graciousness, power and ability) But if it is by grace, it is no longer conditioned on works or anything men have done. Otherwise, grace would no longer be grace (it would be meaningless).

2. 11:7 - Israel failed to obtain what it sought (God's favor by obedience to the Law). Only the elect (those chosen few) obtained it, while the rest of them became callously indifferent (blinded) hardened, and made insensible to it. As it is written, God gave them a spirit (an attitude) of stupor, eyes that should not see and ears that should not hear (that has continued) down to this very day.

3. 11:11 - Has Israel stumbled so as to fall to their utter spiritual ruin irretrievably? By no means! But through their false step and transgression salvation has come to me, a Gentile (without God).

4. 11:17 - But if some of the branches were broken off, while I, a wild olive shoot, was grafted in among them to share the richness of the root and sap of the olive tree, I will not boast over the branches and pride myself at their expense. It is not me who supports the root (Abraham and the patriarchs), but the root supports me.

5. 11:19–21 - Branches were broken (pruned) off so that I might be grafted in. They were broken off because of their unbelief (their lack of real faith), and I am established through faith (because I do believe). So I will not become proud and conceited, but rather I will stand in awe and be reverently afraid. For if God did not spare the natural

	branches (because of unbelief), neither will He spare me if I am guilty of the same offense.
6.	11:22 - I take note of and appreciate the gracious kindness and the severity of God: Severity toward those who have fallen, but God's gracious kindness to me—provided I continue in His grace and abide in His kindness; otherwise I too will be cut off (pruned away).

Application

Reading:
Read each confession several times slowly. Which confession speaks the loudest in your heart today?

Meditation:
Begin to rehearse that confession in your heart and aloud. Allow the Holy Spirit to bring the Life of the Word of that confession into your heart.

Prayer:
Formulate that confession into a personalized prayer. Pray it back to the Father asking to be changed into the image of the Word by His grace and cause that Word to become productive in your life.

Contemplation:
Take a few moments to be silent in His presence. Focus on Christ and His love for you. Yield yourself in true surrender to the image of His Word that is bringing life to you today. Allow the Holy Spirit to speak to you personally through that word. By grace through faith in the blood of Jesus choose the appropriate response to what is being spoken in your heart.

Week Three–Day Seven
Romans Chapter Eleven

1. 11:29 - God's gifts and His call are irrevocable. (He never withdraws them when once they are given, and He does not change His mind about those to whom He gives His grace or to whom He sends His call.)

2. 11:30–32 - I was once disobedient and rebellious toward God, but now I have obtained His mercy because of Israel's disobedience. So they also, now are being disobedient while I a Gentile, am receiving mercy that they in turn may one day—through the mercy I am enjoying—also receive mercy that they may share the mercy which has been shown to me—through me as a messenger of the Gospel to them. For God has consigned all men to disobedience, only that He may have mercy on them all alike.

3. 11:33–35 - Oh, the depth of the riches and wisdom and knowledge of God! How unfathomable (inscrutable, unsearchable) are His judgments (His decisions)! And how untraceable (mysterious, undiscoverable) are His ways (His method, His paths)! For who has known the mind of The Lord and who has understood His thoughts, or who has ever been His counselor? Or who has first given God anything that he might be paid back or that he could claim recompense?

4. 11:36 - From God and through God and to God are all things. (For all things originate with Him and come from Him; all things live through Him and all things center in and tend to consummate and to end in Him.) To Him be glory forever! Amen (so be it.).

Application

Reading:

Read each confession several times slowly. Which confession speaks the loudest in your heart today?

Meditation:

Begin to rehearse that confession in your heart and aloud. Allow the Holy Spirit to bring the Life of the Word of that confession into your heart.

Prayer:

Formulate that confession into a personalized prayer. Pray it back to the Father asking to be changed into the image of the Word by His grace and cause that Word to become productive in your life.

Contemplation:

Take a few moments to be silent in His presence. Focus on Christ and His love for you. Yield yourself in true surrender to the image of His Word that is bringing life to you today. Allow the Holy Spirit to speak to you personally through that word. By grace through faith in the blood of Jesus choose the appropriate response to what is being spoken in your heart.

Week Four–Day One
Romans Chapter Twelve

1. 12:1 - In view of all the mercies of God, I make a decisive dedication of my body (presenting all my members and faculties) as a living sacrifice, holy (devoted, consecrated) and well pleasing to God, which is my reasonable (rational, intelligent) service and spiritual worship.
2. 12:2 - I will not be conformed to this world (this age), fashioned after and adapted to its external, superficial customs), but I am transformed (changed) by the entire renewal of my mind (by its new ideals and its new attitude), so that I may prove (for myself what is the good and acceptable and perfect will of God, even the thing which is good and acceptable and perfect (in His sight for me).
3. 12:3–5 - I will not estimate or think of myself more highly than I ought (I will not have an exaggerated opinion of my own importance), but I will rate my ability with sober judgment according to the degree of faith apportioned to me by God. For as in one physical body we have many parts (organs, members), and all of these parts do not have the same function or use. So we, numerous as we are, are one body in Christ (the Messiah) and, individually we are parts one of another (mutually dependent on one another).
4. 12:6 - I will use my gifts (faculties, talents, qualities) according to the grace that is given me according the proportion of my faith.
5. 12:9 - My love is sincere (a real thing). I hate what is evil (loathe all ungodliness, turn in horror from wickedness), but I hold fast to that which is good.
6. 12:10 - I love with brotherly affection (as members of one family), giving precedence and showing honor to all other family members.

Application

Reading:

Read each confession several times slowly. Which confession speaks the loudest in your heart today?

Meditation:

Begin to rehearse that confession in your heart and aloud. Allow the Holy Spirit to bring the Life of the Word of that confession into your heart.

Prayer:

Formulate that confession into a personalized prayer. Pray it back to the Father asking to be changed into the image of the Word by His grace and cause that Word to become productive in your life.

Contemplation:

Take a few moments to be silent in His presence. Focus on Christ and His love for you. Yield yourself in true surrender to the image of His Word that is bringing life to you today. Allow the Holy Spirit to speak to you personally through that word. By grace through faith in the blood of Jesus choose the appropriate response to what is being spoken in your heart.

Week Four–Day Two
Romans Chapter Twelve

1. 12:11 - I never lag in zeal or in earnest endeavor; but I am aglow and burning with the Spirit, serving the Lord.
2. 12:12 - I rejoice and exult in hope. I am steadfast and patient in suffering and tribulation; I am constant in prayer.
3. 12:13 - I contribute to the needs of God's people (sharing in the necessities of the saints), and I pursue and practice hospitality.
4. 12:14 - I bless those who persecute me, (who are cruel in their attitude toward me); I bless and do not curse them.
5. 12:15 - I rejoice with those who rejoice (sharing others' joy), and I weep with those who weep (sharing others' grief).
6. 12:16 - I live in harmony with one another. I am not haughty (snobbish, high-minded, exclusive), but I readily adjust myself to (people, things) and I give myself to humble tasks. I never overestimate myself, nor am I wise in my own conceits.
7. 12:17 - I will repay no one evil for evil, but I take thought for what is honest and proper and noble (aiming to be above reproach) in the sight of everyone.
8. 12:18 - If possible, as far as it depends on me, I will live at peace with everyone.
9. 12:19 - I will never avenge myself, but I leave the way open for God's wrath; for it is written, "Vengeance is Mine, I will repay (requite), says the Lord."
10. 12:20 - If my enemy is hungry, I will feed him; if he is thirsty, I will give him drink; for by so doing I will heap burning coals upon his head.
11. 12:21 - I will not let myself be overcome by evil, but I will overcome (master) evil with good.

Application

Reading:

Read each confession several times slowly. Which confession speaks the loudest in your heart today?

Meditation:

Begin to rehearse that confession in your heart and aloud. Allow the Holy Spirit to bring the Life of the Word of that confession into your heart.

Prayer:

Formulate that confession into a personalized prayer. Pray it back to the Father asking to be changed into the image of the Word by His grace and cause that Word to become productive in your life.

Contemplation:

Take a few moments to be silent in His presence. Focus on Christ and His love for you. Yield yourself in true surrender to the image of His Word that is bringing life to you today. Allow the Holy Spirit to speak to you personally through that word. By grace through faith in the blood of Jesus choose the appropriate response to what is being spoken in your heart.

Week Four–Day Three
Romans Chapter Thirteen

1. 13:1, 2–5—I am loyally subject to the governing (civil) authorities. For there is no authority except from God (by His permission, His sanction), and those that exist do so by God's appointment. Those who resist authority resist what God has appointed and will be bring down judgment upon them selves (receiving the penalty due them). Therefore, I must be subject not only to avoid God's wrath and escape punishment, but also as a matter of principle and for the sake of conscience.

2. 13:7—I will render to all men their dues: pay taxes, to whom taxes are due, revenue to whom revenue is due, respect to whom respect is due, and honor to whom honor is due.

3. 13:8—I will get out of debt and keep out of debt, owing no man anything except love, for if I love my neighbor (if I practice loving others), I have fulfilled the Law (relating to my fellowmen, meeting all its requirements).

4. 13:9—All the commandments: I shall not commit adultery, I shall not kill, I shall not steal, I shall not covet (have an evil desire), and any other commandment, are summed up in the single command—I shall love my neighbor as I love myself.

5. 13:10—Love does no wrong to one's neighbor (it never hurts anybody). Therefore, love meets all the requirement and is the fulfilling of the Law.

6. 13:11–12—I know what a critical hour this is, how it is high time now for me to awake up out of my sleep (rouse to reality). For salvation (final deliverance) is nearer to me now than when I first believed (adhered to, trusted in, and relied on Christ, the Messiah). The night is far gone, and the day is almost here. I will drop and fling away the works and deeds of darkness and put on the full armor of light.

7. 13:13—I will live and conduct myself honorably and becomingly as in the (open light of) day, not in reveling (carousing) and drunkenness, not in immorality and debauchery (sensuality and licentiousness), not in quarreling and jealousy.
8. 13:14—I will clothe myself with the Lord Jesus Christ (the Messiah) and make no provision for (indulging) the flesh (put a stop to thinking about the evil cravings my physical nature) to gratify its desires (lusts).

Application

Reading:
Read each confession several times slowly. Which confession speaks the loudest in your heart today?

Meditation:
Begin to rehearse that confession in your heart and aloud. Allow the Holy Spirit to bring the Life of the Word of that confession into your heart.

Prayer:
Formulate that confession into a personalized prayer. Pray it back to the Father asking to be changed into the image of the Word by His grace and cause that Word to become productive in your life.

Contemplation:
Take a few moments to be silent in His presence. Focus on Christ and His love for you. Yield yourself in true surrender to the image of His Word that is bringing life to you today. Allow the Holy Spirit to speak to you personally through that word. By grace through faith in the blood of Jesus choose the appropriate response to what is being spoken in your heart.

Week Four–Day Four
Romans Chapter Fourteen

1. 14:1–4 - As for the man who is a weak believer, I will welcome him into my fellowship, not to criticize his opinions or pass judgment on his scruples or perplex him with discussions. Who am I to pass judgment on and censure another's household? It is before his own master he stands or falls. And He shall stand and be upheld, for the Master (the Lord) is mighty to support him and make him stand.

2. 14:7–9 - None of us lives to himself (but to the Lord), and none of us dies to himself (but to the Lord), for If I live, I live to the Lord, and if I die, I die to the Lord, So then, whether I live or I die, I belong to the Lord. For Christ died and lived again for this very purpose, that He might be Lord both of the dead and the living.

3. 14:10–13 - Why should I criticize and pass judgment on my brother? Or why should I look down upon or despise my brother? For we shall all stand before the judgment seat of God, for it is written, "As I live, says the Lord, every knee shall bow to Me, and every tongue shall confess to God (acknowledge Him to His honor and to His praise)." So each of us shall give an account of himself or herself. I will no more criticize and blame and pass judgment on another, but rather I will decide and endeavor never to put a stumbling block or an obstacle or a hindrance in the way of a brother.

Application

Reading:
Read each confession several times slowly. Which confession speaks the loudest in your heart today?

Meditation:
Begin to rehearse that confession in your heart and aloud. Allow the Holy Spirit to bring the Life of the Word of that confession into your heart.

Prayer:
Formulate that confession into a personalized prayer. Pray it back to the Father asking to be changed into the image of the Word by His grace and cause that Word to become productive in your life.

Contemplation:
Take a few moments to be silent in His presence. Focus on Christ and His love for you. Yield yourself in true surrender to the image of His Word that is bringing life to you today. Allow the Holy Spirit to speak to you personally through that word. By grace through faith in the blood of Jesus choose the appropriate response to what is being spoken in your heart.

Week Four–Day Five
Romans Chapter Fourteen

1. 14:14–18 - I know and am convinced as one in the Lord Jesus, that nothing is unclean (forbidden as essentially unclean, defiled, and unholy) of itself, but it is unclean to anyone who things it is unclean. But if my brother is being pained or his feelings hurt or if he is being injured by what I eat, (then) I am no longer walking in love. I will not let what I eat, hurt or cause the ruin of one for whom Christ died. I will not let what seems good to me be considered an evil thing by someone else. (In other words, I will not give occasion for others to criticize that, which is justifiable for me). After all the kingdom of God is not a matter of getting the food and drink I like, but instead it is righteousness, peace and joy by the Holy Spirit. If I serve Christ in this way, I am acceptable and pleasing to God and approved by men.

2. 14:19 - I am definitely aiming for and eagerly pursuing what makes for harmony and for mutual upbuilding (edification and development) of others.

3. 14:20–21 - I must not, for the sake of food, undo and break down and destroy the work of God! Everything is indeed ceremonially clean and pure, but it is wrong for me to hurt the conscience of others or to make them fall by what I eat. The right thing is to eat no meat or drink no wine at all or do anything else if it makes my brother stumble or hurts his conscience or offends or weakens him.

4. 14:22 - I exercise my personal convictions in the presence of God, keeping them to myself (striving only to know the truth and obey His will). I am blessed (happy, to be envied) when I know I have no reason to judge myself by what I approve (I do not convict myself for what I choose to do). But the man who has doubts (misgivings, an uneasy conscience) about eating and then eats (perhaps because of me), stands condemned before God because he

is not true to his convictions and does not act from faith. For whatever does not originate and proceed from faith is sin (whatever is done without a conviction of its approval by God is sinful).

Application

Reading:
Read each confession several times slowly. Which confession speaks the loudest in your heart today?

Meditation:
Begin to rehearse that confession in your heart and aloud. Allow the Holy Spirit to bring the Life of the Word of that confession into your heart.

Prayer:
Formulate that confession into a personalized prayer. Pray it back to the Father asking to be changed into the image of the Word by His grace and cause that Word to become productive in your life.

Contemplation:
Take a few moments to be silent in His presence. Focus on Christ and His love for you. Yield yourself in true surrender to the image of His Word that is bringing life to you today. Allow the Holy Spirit to speak to you personally through that word. By grace through faith in the blood of Jesus choose the appropriate response to what is being spoken in your heart.

Week Four–Day Six
Romans Chapter Fifteen

1. 15:1 - We who are strong in our convictions and of robust faith ought to bear with the failings and the frailties and the tender scruples of the weak, (we ought to help carry the doubts and qualms of others) and not to please ourselves.

2. 15:2 - I will make it a practice to please my neighbor for his good and for his true welfare, to edify him (to strengthen him and build him up spiritually). For Christ did not please Himself (gave no thought to His own interests); but, as it is written, "The approaches and abuses of those who reproached and abused you fell on Me."

3. 15:3–4 - Whatever was thus written in former days was written for my instruction, that by my steadfast and patient endurance and the encouragement drawn from the Scriptures, I might hold fast to and cherish hope.

4. 15:5–6 - Now may the God Who gives the power of patient endurance (steadfastness) and Who supplies encouragement, grant me to live in such mutual harmony and such full sympathy with others, in accord with Christ Jesus, that together we may (unanimously) with united hearts and one voice praise and glorify the God and Father of our Lord Jesus Christ (the Messiah).

5. 15:7 - I will welcome and receive others even as Christ has welcomed and received me for the glory of God.

6. 15:13 - The God of my hope will so fill me with all joy and peace in believing (through the experience of my faith that by the power of the Holy Spirit), I may abound and be overflowing (bubbling over) with hope.

7. 15:14 - I am rich in goodness, amply filled with all spiritual knowledge and competent to admonish and counsel and instruct others also.

8. 15:18 - Christ works through me as an instrument in His hands to win obedience from the Gentiles (without God), by word and deed, even as my preaching is accompanied with the power of signs and wonders, and all of it by the power of the Holy Spirit.
9. 15:29 - I come to you in the abundant blessing of the Gospel of Christ.

Application

Reading:

Read each confession several times slowly. Which confession speaks the loudest in your heart today?

Meditation:

Begin to rehearse that confession in your heart and aloud. Allow the Holy Spirit to bring the Life of the Word of that confession into your heart.

Prayer:

Formulate that confession into a personalized prayer. Pray it back to the Father asking to be changed into the image of the Word by His grace and cause that Word to become productive in your life.

Contemplation:

Take a few moments to be silent in His presence. Focus on Christ and His love for you. Yield yourself in true surrender to the image of His Word that is bringing life to you today. Allow the Holy Spirit to speak to you personally through that word. By grace through faith in the blood of Jesus choose the appropriate response to what is being spoken in your heart.

Week Four–Day Seven
Romans Chapter Sixteen

1. 16:17—I am on my guard concerning those who create dissensions and difficulties and cause divisions, in opposition to the doctrine (the teaching), which I have been taught.
2. 16:19—My loyalty and obedience is known to all. I am well versed and wise as to what is good and innocent and I am guileless as to what is evil.
3. 16:20—The God of peace will soon crush Satan under my feet. The grace of the Lord Jesus Christ (the Messiah) is with me.
4. 16:25–26—God is able to strengthen me in the faith which is according to the gospel concerning Jesus Christ (the Messiah), according to the revelation (the unveiling) of the mystery of the plan of redemption which was kept in silence and secret for long ages, but is now disclosed and through the prophetic Scriptures is made known to all nations, according to the command of the eternal God, (to win them) to obedience to the faith.
5. 16:27—To the only wise God be glory forevermore through Jesus Christ (the Anointed One)! Amen!

Application

Reading:
Read each confession several times slowly. Which confession speaks the loudest in your heart today?

Meditation:
Begin to rehearse that confession in your heart and aloud. Allow the Holy Spirit to bring the Life of the Word of that confession into your heart.

Prayer:
Formulate that confession into a personalized prayer. Pray it back to the Father asking to be changed into the image of the Word by His grace and cause that Word to become productive in your life.

Contemplation:
Take a few moments to be silent in His presence. Focus on Christ and His love for you. Yield yourself in true surrender to the image of His Word that is bringing life to you today. Allow the Holy Spirit to speak to you personally through that word. By grace through faith in the blood of Jesus choose the appropriate response to what is being spoken in your heart.

The Ten Commandments

Old Testament
Exodus 20:1–17

20:1 "And God spoke all these words, saying: 'I am the LORD your God, who brought you out of the land of Egypt, out of the house of bondage.'"

1. "You shall have no other gods before Me."
2. "You shall not make for yourself a carved image, or any likeness of anything that is in heaven above, or that is in the earth beneath, or that is in the water under the earth; you shall not bow down to them nor serve them. For I, the LORD your God, am a jealous God, visiting the iniquity of the fathers on the children to the third and fourth generations of those who hate Me, but showing mercy to thousands, to those who love Me and keep My commandments."
3. "You shall not take the name of the LORD your God in vain, for the LORD will not hold him guiltless who takes His name in vain."
4. "Remember the Sabbath day, to keep it holy. Six days you shall labor and do all your work, but the seventh day is the Sabbath of the LORD your God. In it you shall do no work: you, nor your son, nor your daughter, nor your male servant, nor your female servant, nor your cattle, nor your stranger who is within your gates. For in six days the LORD made the heavens and the earth, the sea, and all that is in them, and rested the seventh day. Therefore the LORD blessed the Sabbath day and hallowed it."
5. "Honor your father and your mother, that your days may be long upon the land which the LORD your God is giving you."

6. "You shall not murder."
7. "You shall not commit adultery."
8. "You shall not steal."
9. "You shall not bear false witness against your neighbor.'
10. "You shall not covet your neighbor's house; you shall not covet your neighbor's wife, nor his male servant, nor his female servant, nor his ox, nor his donkey, nor anything that is your neighbor's."

Two Commandments

New Testament
Matthew 22:36–40

"Teacher, which is the great commandment in the law?" Jesus said to him:

1. 'You shall love the LORD your God with all your heart, with all your soul, and with all your mind.' This is the first and great commandment.
2. And the second is like it: 'You shall love your neighbor as yourself.'

"On these two commandments hang all the Law and the Prophets."

Contact Information

Contact Sharolyn Sidebottom or order more copies
of this book at

TATE PUBLISHING, LLC

127 East Trade Center Terrace
Mustang, Oklahoma 73064

(888) 361 - 9473

TATE PUBLISHING, LLC

www.tatepublishing.com